"Bringing Asia to the World"™

趣学中文

Go Far WITH CHINESE

Textbook 1A

Senior Curriculum Adviser

Ying Jin 金璎

Lead Instructional Contributors

Cilei Han 韩慈磊

Zoey Liu 刘喆医

Diane Neubauer 杜雁子

Erica Pollard 狄瑞和

CHENG & TSUI

"Bringing Asia to the World"™

First Edition 2020

23 22 21 20 19   1 2 3 4 5

ISBN 978-1-62291-476-0 [First Edition]

Library of Congress Cataloging in Publication data applied for.

Printed in Canada

The *Go Far with Chinese* series encompasses textbooks, workbooks, teacher's resources, audio, video, and more. Visit cheng-tsui.com for more information on the other components of *Go Far with Chinese*.

Publisher
JILL CHENG

Curriculum Development Manager
MEGAN BURNETT

Curriculum Development Staff
LEI WANG, TAMSIN TRUE-ALCALA, EMILY PETIT, YINGCHUN GUAN

Managing Editor
KAESMENE HARRISON BANKS

Market and Photo Researchers
ELIZABETH HANLON, MARIAN STACEY

Cover Designers
CHRISTIAN SABOGAL with MARINA LI

Interior Designers
KATE PAPADAKI with MARINA LI

Comic Illustrator
MARGARET LOR

Photographs
© Adobe Stock
© Cheng & Tsui
© Shutterstock
© iStock

Photo credits are listed on p. 227

Cheng & Tsui Company, Inc.
25 West Street, Boston, MA 02111-1213 USA
P: 617.988.2400 / 800.554.1963
F: 617.426.3669
cheng-tsui.com

Series Contributors

Senior Curriculum Adviser

Ying Jin (金瓔) is a Chinese teacher in the Fremont Union High School District in California. She has more than 20 years of experience in Chinese instruction and is active in the teaching community through STARTALK, CLASS, California Language Teachers' Association, and more. In 2018, ACTFL named her the National Language Teacher of the Year, the first Chinese language teacher to receive this honor. She is passionate about promoting greater understanding of Chinese language and culture.

Lead Instructional Contributors

Cilei Han (韩慈磊) is a teacher of Chinese language at Lake Oswego and Lakeridge High Schools in Oregon as well as a Challenge Program instructor at Portland State University. She serves as a board member of the Chinese Language Teachers Association, USA (CLTA-US), as chair of the CLTA K-12 Working Group, and as president of her regional Chinese Language Teachers Association-Oregon. She is dedicated to assisting in the development of stronger K-12 Chinese language programs nationwide.

Zoey Liu (刘喆医) teaches Chinese in the Fremont Union High School District in California. In 2017, she received the Yao Memorial Award for Outstanding New Teacher from CLASS. She is committed to helping students grow as global citizens by deepening their knowledge of Chinese language and culture.

Diane Neubauer (杜雁子), currently a PhD student in Foreign Language and ESL Education at the University of Iowa, has more than a decade of experience teaching Chinese at both elementary and secondary schools. She frequently conducts professional development workshops for language teachers and works to support and develop the community of Chinese teachers through her role as vice-chair of the ACTFL Comprehension-based Communicative Language Teaching Special Interest Group. She also regularly blogs about ideas and strategies for teaching Chinese.

Erica Pollard (狄瑞和) is the foreign language department director and an AP®[1] Chinese instructor at Hingham Public Schools in Massachusetts. She has extensive experience in curriculum design and has developed curricula for Chinese language courses from beginner to AP® levels. She also shares her teaching insights and knowledge through her work on the College Board's AP® Chinese Language and Culture Development Committee.

[1]AP® is a trademark registered by the College Board, which is not affiliated with, and does not endorse, this product.

Publisher's Note

Over the last four decades, Cheng & Tsui has grown from a scrappy distribution operation into a leading publisher of Chinese, Japanese, Korean, and Arabic language and culture materials, introducing Asia not only to America, but also to the rest of the world. We want to thank all of you, the many dedicated authors, staff, educators, and learners, who have made this milestone anniversary possible.

While we look back on past achievements — like the 1997 publication of the first edition of the global bestseller *Integrated Chinese*, followed by *Adventures in Japanese* in 1998 — we also look forward to a bright future. Over the years, trusting in our commitment to innovative, effective, and high quality language pedagogy, many educators have asked us for a new beginning Chinese textbook series for secondary school students. On our 40th anniversary, we are excited to answer this call with *Go Far with Chinese!*

You told us that you want a new textbook series that

- is innovative and effective;
- is age-appropriate, thematically-organized, and proficiency-based;
- offers careful vocabulary and grammar control;
- is designed with appropriate pacing and thoughtful articulation;
- provides robust support for teachers and students with authentic materials;
- is informed by the most current research on best practices in second language acquisition;
- is based on real classroom experiences of teachers and students; and
- promises to lead new generations on a lifelong path to Chinese language learning!

In planning for such an ambitious project, we sought the advice and participation of outstanding teachers, researchers, and learners throughout America. Collaborating closely with our many advisers, Cheng & Tsui's highly dedicated and thoughtful curriculum development staff have made your requests a reality in *Go Far with Chinese!*

We know that it is difficult for any single textbook to meet the needs of every different kind of student audience and classroom setting. But as you use this material, we hope you will find that *Go Far with Chinese* provides enough structure and flexibility to make teaching easier and students' learning more fun and effective.

We truly believe that your success is our success, so we ask that you continue to let us know what you need and what you have on your wishlist. Only with your input can we continue to develop materials that will help you achieve your goals. Please contact your Cheng & Tsui account representative or editor@cheng-tsui.com with your suggestions.

All of us at Cheng & Tsui are grateful for your support!

Acknowledgments

Go Far with Chinese was developed thanks to the advice and contributions of countless educators from all across the United States. We would like to express our gratitude and appreciation to all those who contributed, including those listed below.

何仲健
Carol Bi
Boulder Creek High School
Anthem, Arizona

常小林
Xiaolin Chang, M.A.
Consultant to College Board AP®[2] Chinese, former Chair of the Language Department
Lowell High School
San Francisco, California

趙哲瑩
Che-Ying Joy Chao
Woodbridge High School
Irvine, California

姜文静
Wenching Chiang
Sunset Ridge Middle School
East Hartford, Connecticut

董昕
Xin Dong, M.A.
Lincoln-Sudbury Regional High School
Sudbury, Massachusetts

簡淑玲
Shwuling Jane
Jonas Clarke Middle School
Lexington, Massachusetts

景晓姝
Xiaoshu Jing, M.A.
Marlborough High School
Marlborough, Massachusetts

林玫
Mary Lane, M.A.
Tenafly Public Schools (retired)
Tenafly, New Jersey

李宜
Yi Lee
Henry J. Kaiser High School
Honolulu, Hawaii

李娜
Na Li, M.A.
Chinese Teacher and World Language Curriculum Coordinator
Columbus Academy
Gahanna, Ohio

林静容
Janet Lin
St. Mark's School of Texas
Dallas, Texas

刘兵
Bing Liu, M.A.
Metropolitan Learning Center
Bloomfield, Connecticut

刘伟
Wei Liu, PhD
The Hotchkiss School
Lakeville, Connecticut

卢文雅
Wenya Lu, M.A.
Teacher and Curriculum Developer
Northside College Preparatory High School
Chicago, Illinois

陳惠棻
Petra Lynch
Greenhill High School
Addison, Texas

秦莉杰
Lijie Qin, M.A.
Oak Hill Middle School
Newton, Massachusetts

芮尚勤
Dr. Reed Riggs
Brigham Young University–Hawaii

史迪菲
Difei Shi
Tenakill Middle School
Closter, New Jersey

孙毅
Preston Sundin, M.A.
Emma Willard School
Troy, New York

吴萍
Ping Wu, M.Ed.
Columbus School for Girls
Columbus, Ohio

赖华睿
Reid Wyatt, M.A.T.
Brooks School
North Andover, Massachusetts

薛莉
Li Xue, M.A.
Wainwright Intermediate School
Fircrest, Washington

张世红
Shihong Zhang, M.A. & M.Ed.
Glen Ridge High School
Glen Ridge, New Jersey

[1]All Chinese names are listed in accordance with the way they were provided.

[2]AP® is a trademark registered by the College Board, which is not affiliated with, and does not endorse, this product.

Contents

Unit 2: Exploring a New Place

Chapter 4: Goodbye America, Hello China!

Chapter 5: Sports in the Neighborhood

Chapter 6: Appreciating New Sounds

Unit 3: Celebrating Special Occasions

Chapter 7: Do You Have Plans?

Chapter 8: Shopping for the Perfect Gift

Chapter 9: A Birthday Dinner

Preface

The origins of *Go Far with Chinese* are firmly rooted in the experience of Chinese teachers and students at the secondary school level. The series covers three to four years of beginning Chinese language instruction in a traditional U.S. secondary school setting. Levels 1A and 1B teach the same content as Level 1, but are designed to be used for two years at the middle school level or in high school programs with fewer instructional hours. Students who complete the three-level series will be ready to study Integrated Chinese Volumes 3 and 4 either for AP®[3] preparation or at the college level. Upon completing Level 1A, students will be able to confidently embark on their own language learning journeys.

Foundational Ideas

The curriculum of *Go Far with Chinese* was developed in accordance with the best practices defined by current research in second language acquisition. In particular, the curriculum is fully aligned to the World-Readiness Standards and Guiding Principles for Language Learning recommended by the American Council on the Teaching of Foreign Languages (ACTFL). Below are some of the foundational ideas that shaped the program.

Proficiency-Based Instruction

Go Far with Chinese places strong emphasis on real-world communication—that is, on what students can actually *do* with the language they have learned. Using a backward design process, the curriculum development team first identified language and cultural content learning goals, and then used those goals to write the comic stories at the end of each Chapter. The team then outlined Unit-level Integrated Performance Assessments and worked with expert Chinese language educators from across the United States to plan the task-based learning experiences and instructional materials that would help students reach those goals.

Vocabulary Control

Careful attention was paid to vocabulary control. High-frequency "function" words, such as 想, 喜欢, and 去, are introduced early to give students the ability to have authentic conversations about their likes, wants, and plans. In addition, the program also prioritizes relevant vocabulary, such as words related to pets, families, sports, and music.

Grammar in Context

Current research indicates that the most effective method for teaching grammar is to present it in context, focusing on the communicative meaning of a form rather than on explaining the form itself. In the Textbook, students are encouraged to get the gist of the meaning of new language before focusing on the details of form.

[3]AP® is a trademark registered by the College Board, which is not affiliated with, and does not endorse, this product.

Emphasis on Meaning-Based Tasks & Activities

Go Far with Chinese emphasizes authentic communicative tasks that ask students to express ideas and opinions, rather than formulaic drills or rehearsed exercises. Practice sections in the Textbook move from brief, semi-guided exercises to independent tasks structured to elicit meaning-based communication.

Literacy & Character Learning

While literacy instruction should be an integral part of any beginning Chinese program, there is also a clear need to set realistic goals given the challenges of learning a new writing system. *Go Far with Chinese* is designed to support literacy instruction while giving teachers flexibility with regard to writing assignments. For example, students are expected to learn to read and write only the words in the vocabulary lists, while word banks throughout the Textbook provide supplemental vocabulary. Pinyin is provided for new words and then phased out over the course of each Section to help students develop strong reading skills. To accelerate students' word recognition, *Go Far with Chinese* explicitly teaches the recurring components and stroke order of Chinese characters. Open-ended questions in the Textbook and Workbook allow teachers to let their students either handwrite or type their responses.

Use of Target Language

To help achieve ACTFL's goal for teachers to conduct 90% of classroom learning time in the target language, *Go Far with Chinese* teaches students useful classroom phrases early on. Additional comprehensible input strategies provided in the Teacher's Resources also help maximize students' exposure to Chinese during class time.

Personalization

In order to increase student interest and create opportunities for real-world communication, activities and exercises were designed to relate to students' lives and to encourage them to express their own ideas and opinions. Additionally, the Teacher's Resources suggest ways to tap into students' specific interests and adapt classroom content accordingly.

Stories as a Teaching Tool

The final Section of each Chapter combines the new language students have studied in an engaging comic story. Age- and level-appropriate plots foster student interest and engagement. The stories in *Go Far with Chinese* are presented in dialogue format to keep the focus on informal spoken language and to model natural exchanges.

Authentic Materials

The ACTFL Guiding Principles for Language Learning encourage the use of authentic materials even in the beginning stage of language learning. The realia, photographs and videos of China help build students' cultural literacy. Simple interpretive tasks further enable students to develop their ability to analyze authentic materials.

References

Adair-Hauck, Bonnie, Eileen W. Glisan, and Francis J. Troyan. *Implementing Integrated Performance Assessment.* Alexandria, VA: American Council on the Teaching of Foreign Languages, 2013.

Clementi, Donna, and Laura Terrill. *The Keys to Planning for Learning, Second Edition.* Alexandria, VA: American Council on the Teaching of Foreign Languages, 2017.

"Guiding Principles for Language Learning." The American Council on the Teaching of Foreign Languages. Accessed August 6, 2019. https://www.actfl.org/guiding-principles

Hadley, Alice Omaggio. *Teaching Language in Context, Third Edition.* Boston: Heinle & Heinle, 2001.

Mart, Cagri. "Teaching Grammar in Context: Why and How?" *Theory and Practice in Language Studies* Vol. 3, No. 1 (2013): 124-129.

Rezende Lucarevschi, Claudio. "The Role of Storytelling on Language Learning: A Literature Review." *Working Papers of the Linguistic Circle of the University of Victoria* Vol. 26, No. 1 (2016): 23-44

VanPatten, Bill. *While We're On the Topic.* Alexandria, VA: American Council on the Teaching of Foreign Languages, 2017.

Wong, Wynn and Bill VanPatten. "The Evidence is IN: Drills are OUT." *Foreign Language Annals* Vol. 36, No. 3 (2003): 403-423.

Waltz, Terry. *TPRS with Chinese Characteristics.* Squid for Brains Educational Publishing, 2015.

Textbook Organization

Each Level in *Go Far with Chinese* includes a Textbook, Workbook, Character Workbook, audio, video, and Teacher's Resources.

Level 1A is divided into three thematic Units consisting of three Chapters each. In every Unit, a broad, thought-provoking Essential Question challenges students to reflect on how they view language, their own culture and other cultures, and the world at large. Unit Projects, in the form of Integrated Performance Assessments (IPAs), test students' ability to understand and use the language they have learned in a real-world scenario.

Each Chapter of *Go Far with Chinese* follows a tiered approach to instruction: students move from processing teacher-provided comprehensible input to brief, semi-guided exercises, and finally to independent tasks. To keep the pace manageable, the target vocabulary and grammar are divided and introduced over the first three Sections of each Chapter. The fourth and final Section, Put the Pieces Together, combines the Chapter's new vocabulary and grammar into a comic story and provides additional projects to round out the Chapter.

Can-Do Goals

Each Chapter begins with Can-Do Goals to set clear expectations for what students will learn to do in the three modes of communication. The Can-Do Goals are restated at the end of each Chapter for students to check their own progress and to take ownership of their learning.

Culture Connection

This feature opens a window into contemporary Chinese culture, highlighting cultural products and practices that influence the daily lives of students' Chinese peers. Relatable and interesting subjects, full-color authentic photographs, topical words and expressions, and reflection questions help students explore the Unit's Essential Question and build intercultural competence.

Language Model [Target Language Input]

Teachers can use the images on the Language Model pages in conjunction with the PowerPoint presentation in the Teacher's Resources to lead a class discussion that makes use of the new structures and vocabulary of the Section. This ensures that students' exposure to the new language comes in a meaningful context through comprehensible input.

New Words in Conversation [Interpretive]

In New Words in Conversation, the Section's vocabulary and grammar are presented in a single, cohesive dialogue. Students first listen to the dialogue and try to grasp the gist of the meaning based on the language input they received during the Language Model discussion. Then, with the aid of the pinyin text and vocabulary list, they read the dialogue, deepening their comprehension and connecting the new language to its written form.

Puzzle It Out [Progress Check]

Students complete these exercises to check their comprehension of the language points presented in Language Model and New Words in Conversation.

Language Reference

Clear explanations, presented alongside helpful visuals, serve as a reference for students to consult to clarify and consolidate their understanding of new grammar and word usage. The language points are presented contextually as ways to convey meaning, rather than as rules to be memorized.

Using the Language [Interpersonal/Presentational]

Interactive tasks elicit spontaneous, unscripted conversation between students by creating situations with a genuine communicative need. Some Using the Language activities are designed to be followed by a class discussion, giving students an opportunity to speak presentationally on the topic at hand. Others consist of games or puzzles that provide a clear communicative goal to encourage interaction.

Put the Pieces Together!

In the final Section, students first read a comic that combines the new language of the Chapter in a single, engaging story. Then, students complete additional exercises covering all three modes of communication to consolidate their grasp of Chapter content and to prepare for the Unit level IPA. Each Put the Pieces Together Section features an exercise built on authentic materials as well as a final project that asks students to work collaboratively on a presentational performance or piece of writing. In addition, the following three floating features appear at least once in each Chapter.

Language Challenge

The Language Challenge gives motivated and more advanced students an additional opportunity to apply their new language skills and personalize their learning. Teachers can use the Language Challenge as extra credit or as a way to differentiate instruction, providing an activity for advanced or heritage students who are moving more quickly than their peers.

5Cs

This feature expands on topics that emerge in the Chapter, integrating the 5Cs into the flow of language instruction and helping teachers effectively implement the ACTFL World-Readiness Standards for Language Learning.

What a Character!

Students are introduced to common radicals and character components that appear in some words in a Chapter, resulting in an integrated, context-driven foray into character analysis.

Scope & Sequence

Unit 1: First Impressions

Essential Question: How do we form first impressions?

Chapter	Can-Do Goals	Language Points
Chapter 1: Getting to Know Chinese Culture Connection: China 中国	Learn about: • Different Chinese dialects • Chinese characters • Pinyin • The structure of simple Chinese sentences Learn to: • Greet someone in Chinese • Create simple sentences in Chinese • Understand some words and phrases for the classroom • Write the numbers one through ten in Chinese characters	• Basic word order • Asking questions with 吗 • Negative word 不
Chapter 2: What's in a Name? Culture Connection: Names 名字	• Understand how Chinese names are different from English names • Tell others your name • Ask for someone's name • Say that something belongs to someone • Respond to "what" and "who" questions • Express that you have or do not have something	• Indicating possession with 的 • Using question words such as 什么 • Expressing having and not having with 有 and 没有 • Using the connecting words 和 and 也
Chapter 3: Tell Me About Yourself Culture Connection: Family 家庭	• Understand simple descriptions of families • Ask and answer questions about family members • Express how many siblings and pets you have • Understand when others talk about their likes and dislikes • Talk about likes and dislikes • Use different measure words to talk about people and animals	• Using measure words such as 个 • Asking questions using the A不A pattern • Action word + Action word • Expressing degree with 很，不太，and 不 • Measure words for animals (只，条，匹)

Unit 2: Exploring a New Place

Essential Question: How does where you live affect what you do?

Chapter	Can-Do Goals	Language Points
Chapter 4: Goodbye America, Hello China! Culture Connection: Beijing, My Hometown 北京，我的老家	• Describe something that two or more people have in common • Understand where someone is and say where you are • Ask someone to make a choice between two options • Use "this" and "that" to refer to things if you do not know the words in Chinese • Talk about your location now and your location this week	• Using 都 to say "all" or "both" • Pointing things out with 这 and 那 • Using 还是 to prompt a choice • Verbal use of 在 • Word order with time expressions
Chapter 5: Sports in the Neighborhood Culture Connection: Sports & Exercise 体育运动	• Name some sports that are popular in China • Discuss which sports you can play • Say where you play sports • Express whether or not you want to play a sport • Understand the sports others can and want to play • Ask if others want to play or watch sports	• Use of 会 to say what you can do • Different verbs for playing sports • Using 有 to show existence • 很 + predicate • Prepositional 在
Chapter 6: Appreciating New Sounds Culture Connection: Music 音乐	• Recognize some traditional Chinese musical instruments and their sounds • Understand when others talk about playing different kinds of instruments • Say which instruments you play or want to learn to play • Offer to teach someone to play an instrument, and say who teaches you • Understand how the words 呢, 啊, and 吧 change the meaning or tone of a sentence	• Different verbs for playing instruments • Using 啊，吧，and 呢 • Using the verb 教 • 会 versus 可以

Unit 3: Celebrating Special Occasions

Essential Questions: What makes a day special?

Chapter	Can-Do Goals	Language Points
Chapter 7: Do You Have Plans? Culture Connection: Special Occasions 庆贺	• State the date and the day of the week of an upcoming activity • Understand numbers larger than ten • Discuss when you are free • Ask and answer questions about birthdays • Talk about buying a gift based on someone's interests	• Days of the week • Numbers 11–99 • Giving specific dates • Responding to new information with 那
Chapter 8: Shopping for the Perfect Gift Culture Connection: Giving Gifts 送礼物	• Understand when others describe what they are going to do • Talk about when you are busy and when you plan to do certain activities • Use appropriate greetings for phone conversations • Agree or disagree with someone • Discuss purchasing a gift for someone • Give simple descriptions of books and clothes	• Expressing wants and intentions with 要 • Time + 见 • Adding description with 而且 • Linking descriptions to nouns with 的
Chapter 9: A Birthday Dinner Culture Connection: Special Dishes 美食	• Talk about things you do for others • Name some Chinese dishes and say what foods you like • Recognize some Chinese holiday foods • Learn to order food from a restaurant • Discuss completed actions • State opinions and give reasons	• 好 + verb • Using 给 to add direction to other verbs • Using 了 for completed actions • Giving a reason with 因为……所以……

This icon indicates that audio content is available. Audio can be downloaded at cheng-tsui.com.

FIRST IMPRESSIONS

In Unit 1, you will learn how to introduce yourself in Chinese. You will also learn how to ask and answer questions in Chinese about family, pets, and interests.

UNIT 1

第 dì
一 yī
单 dān
元 yuán

Essential Question

How do we form first impressions?

CHAPTER 1
Getting to Know Chinese

Emma, Isabella, and Martin Lopez are moving to Beijing! What kind of place is China?

CHAPTER 2
What's in a Name?

Isabella and Martin both have Chinese names. Learn how they chose them.

CHAPTER 3
Tell Me About Yourself

Martin and Isabella find out Daming has a little brother ... but his little brother doesn't have an older brother?!

UNIT 1 PROJECT

At the end of the unit, you will imagine that a group of exchange students from China is coming to your school. To prepare for their visit, you will:

- Read the exchange students' self-introductions
- Choose an exchange student and prepare to be his or her guide by writing your own letter of self-introduction
- Play a guessing game and try to figure out which exchange student your partner has chosen

Getting to Know Chinese

CHAPTER
1
第 dì
一 yī
课 kè

Sixteen-year-old Isabella and fourteen-year-old Martin Lopez both study Chinese in school. They are about to learn that their mother, Emma, is planning a major change for the family...

Can-Do Goals

In this chapter, you will learn about:

- Different Chinese dialects
- Chinese characters
- Pinyin, a system to sound out Chinese characters
- The structure of simple Chinese sentences

In this chapter, you will also learn to:

- Greet someone in Chinese
- Create simple sentences in Chinese
- Understand some words and phrases for the classroom
- Write the numbers one through ten in Chinese characters

An Adventure for the Lopez Family

5
Yeah! I've always wanted to see the Great Wall! This is going to be awesome!
I don't know...This is so sudden...
6
I know. Here, I got you this book about China. If you learn more about China, it'll be easier for you to adjust when we get there.
CHINA
7
Can you believe this? This is so unfair! This book says the driving age in China is 18. I'm never going to be able to drive!
Beijing is a big city—there are buses and subways. I think it's going to be more exciting than living in this little town.
8
But we'll be leaving our friends! And I'm sure I could have made varsity softball next year.
I bet there will be lots of new things to try in China.
I don't know...
CHINA

Isabella and Martin will experience some major changes this summer. What do you think this would be like? Ask yourself:

1. Do you think that reading a book is a good way to get a first impression of a new place? Why or why not?
2. What other sources of information could help you get to know a place?
3. How would you feel if your parents told you that you would be moving to a different country?

Meet the Neighbors

The Lopezes are moving to a very international neighborhood in Beijing. In addition to Daming, here are some of their new neighbors. Their conversations throughout the book will help introduce you to the Chinese language.

Leo Fischer, 14,
from Germany

Sanjay Patel, 15,
from the United States

Maya Young, 14,
from the United States

Ellen Jones, 16,
from the United Kingdom

Miko Futamura, 16,
from Japan

Owen Kang, 16,
from the United States

Zhōngguó

China

Isabella and Martin were surprised to learn they are moving to China. They didn't know what to think! They read the guidebook their mother bought for them, and what they learned helped them form an impression of their new home. Here are some facts they learned about China from the guidebook.

Approximate border of China

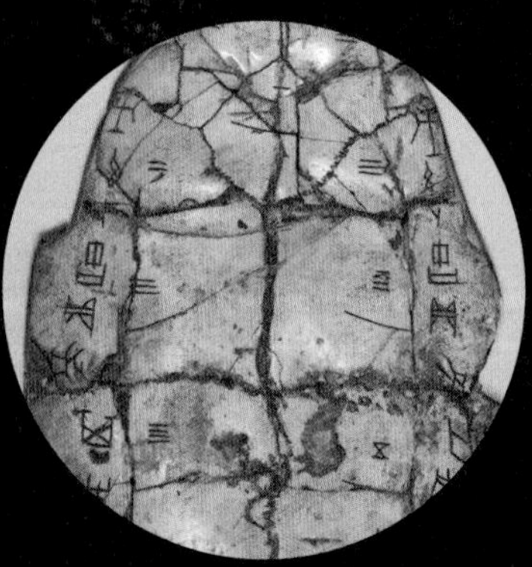

Ancient Chinese writing on a tortoise shell.

An Ancient Culture

Civilization in China can be traced back thousands of years through the history of Chinese characters. The earliest known form of Chinese writing was carved into ox bones and tortoise shells more than 3,000 years ago. There are still some characters in use today that are clearly related to this ancient script.

China Is Big!

China is one of the biggest countries in the world and has the largest population — about 1.4 BILLION people! However, nearly everyone lives in the eastern half of the country, as this photograph of China at night shows.

By the Numbers

Although Chinese culture is ancient, China is also an influential, modern country. It has one of the largest economies in the world and has a permanent seat on the United Nations Security Council. Due to its large population and rapid economic growth, China also ranks first in the world in many categories, such as:

Demand for instant noodles: **38,970,000,000** servings (in 2017).

Electricity consumed: **5.664 trillion** kWh (in 2016).

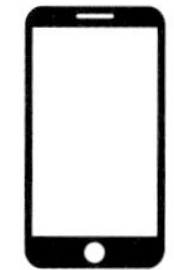

Cell phone subscriptions: **1,474,097,000** (in 2017).

Borders with other countries: **14** (tied with Russia).

High-speed train track: **15,700** miles (in 2017).

Sources: World Instant Noodle Association, 2018; CIA World Factbook, 2018; National Bureau of Statistics, China, 2017.

REFLECT ON THE ESSENTIAL QUESTION

How do we form first impressions?

1. What did you know about China before you read this passage? How has your impression of the country changed?
2. The majority of Chinese people live in a relatively small part of the country. Are people evenly spread across your country or state? Why or why not?
3. What information would you share with people who are planning to visit your town or city? What impression would you want to give them?

Introduction to Chinese

Chinese both looks and sounds quite different from English. Understanding more about these differences will help you learn this fascinating language, which is used by over a billion people around the world.

Spoken Chinese: Many Dialects

There are many dialects of Chinese, and some are so different that speakers of one dialect cannot understand speakers of another! The two Chinese characters 你好 make up the greeting "hello." However, this simple greeting does not sound the same in the different dialects throughout China.

Audio

In Mandarin, these characters are pronounced "nee how."

In the dialect of Shanghai, this greeting sounds like "nong hoh."

In Cantonese, the dialect of Guangzhou, these characters are pronounced "nay hoh."

In this textbook, the dialect you will learn is Standard Modern Chinese, often referred to simply as Chinese or Mandarin. Mandarin is an official language of the People's Republic of China (Mainland China), Taiwan, and Singapore.

Written Chinese: Characters

Most Chinese words are made up of one to three characters. Each character represents a specific meaning and has a one-syllable sound associated with it. This is unlike English, in which letters represent sounds but not meaning. Instead of comparing Chinese characters to the English alphabet, you can compare them to Arabic numerals like 1, 2, and 3. When you see Arabic numerals, you know what they mean and how to say them, even though they aren't spelled out.

Simplified and Traditional Forms

Chinese is written using characters, but there is more than one type of Chinese character. The two main types of modern Chinese characters are often referred to as "simplified" and "traditional." This book uses simplified characters, which were created by the government of the People's Republic of China in the mid-1900s with the hope of making characters easier to learn. However, you will still find the more complex traditional characters in many places, including Hong Kong, Taiwan, and possibly even your local Chinese restaurant!

Simplified
鸭
Appetizers
1. 鹽水鴨 Salted Duck 9.50
2. 五香牛腱 Five Spice Beef Shank 8.50
3. 酸辣黃瓜 Hot and Sour Cucumber 6.00

Comprehension Check

		T	F
1	Standard Chinese is the only dialect spoken in China.	○	○
2	Each Chinese character represents a sound but not a meaning, just like a letter of the English alphabet.	○	○
3	Traditional characters are no longer used.	○	○

Mandarin pronunciation

Young people across China may speak many different dialects, but most of them will learn Mandarin in school. In the mid-1900s, the government of the People's Republic of China developed a spelling system called pinyin to help teach Mandarin to students throughout the country. This system will also help you learn how to pronounce characters.

Pinyin

The pinyin system uses letters to spell out Mandarin sounds. Most characters are spoken as one-syllable sounds. These sounds have three parts: the initial sound, the final sound, and the tone. Special accent marks, called tone marks, show the tone (or pitch) of the syllable. For example, here's the pinyin for the Chinese character 八 (eight):

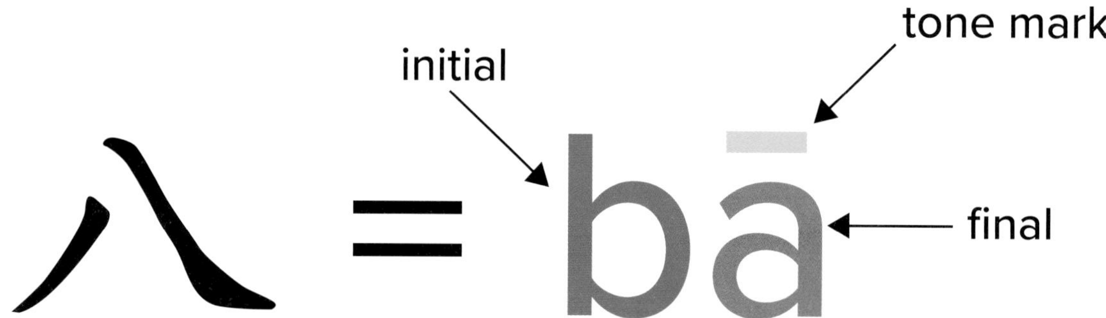

In this example, the initial sound is the consonant b. The final sound is the vowel a, and the tone is represented by the line over the a. The final sound is generally a vowel sound. Most Mandarin syllables do not end in a consonant, and the only possible final consonant sounds are -n, -ng, and -r.

To learn more about pinyin spelling and hear examples of each sound in Mandarin, refer to the Appendix at the end of the book.

Tones

A tone tells you how to pitch your voice as you say a syllable. There are four tones in Mandarin. Tones may be tricky at first, but they are very important, since changing the tone of a syllable changes its meaning. For example, if you say dǎ instead of dà, you'll be saying "to hit" instead of "big."

Here are the four main tones in Mandarin Chinese:

dā	dá	dǎ	dà
First Tone	Second Tone	Third Tone	Fourth Tone

Audio

5
4
3
2
1

In pinyin, the tone mark is located above a vowel sound for each syllable. If you see a syllable in pinyin that has no tone mark, that means it has a neutral tone. A syllable with a neutral tone is said lightly, with no strong emphasis.

Comprehension Check

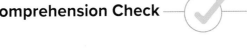

		T	F
1	Pinyin is a system used to help teach Mandarin pronunciation.		
2	Mandarin syllables usually end with a vowel.		
3	Mandarin has a total of three different tones.		

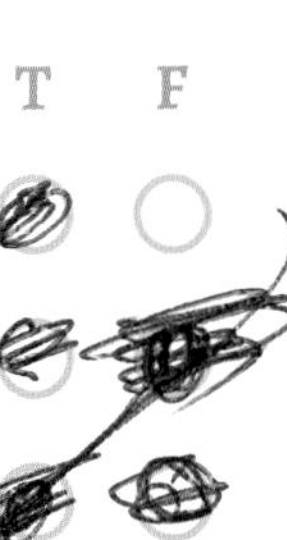

Getting started in Chinese

You've learned some basic information about characters and the different Mandarin sounds that will help you understand Chinese words. The next step is to put words together to create simple sentences and questions.

Basic Word Order

The basic word order for a sentence in English and Chinese is the same: a subject, followed by a verb, and then (sometimes) an object. The subject either does the action of the sentence or is the person or thing described by the sentence. The verb is the word that expresses the action or state of being. In sentences that have an object, the object is the word that is affected by the verb.

Subject	Verb	Object		
Wǒ	xǐhuan	tā		
I	like	it	→	I like it.

Asking Questions

To ask a simple yes/no question in Chinese, just add the word ma at the end of the sentence. You do not need to change the word order of the sentence.

Subject	Verb	Object			
Nǐ	xǐhuan	tā	ma?		
You	like	it	?	→	Do you like it?

Answering Questions

If you want to respond to a question in the positive, a simple way to do so is to repeat the verb in the question.

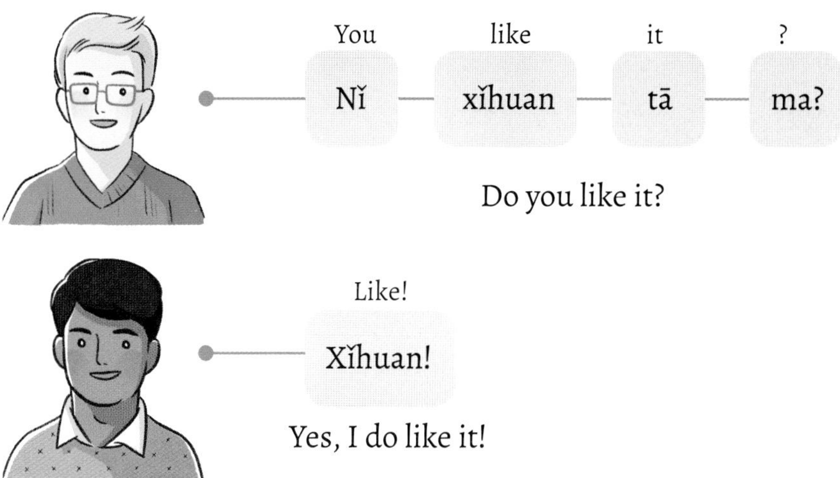

You like it ?
Nǐ xǐhuan tā ma?
Do you like it?
Like!
Xǐhuan!
Yes, I do like it!

If your response is negative, the most common way to answer "no" is to simply add the negative word **bù** (no, not) before the verb.

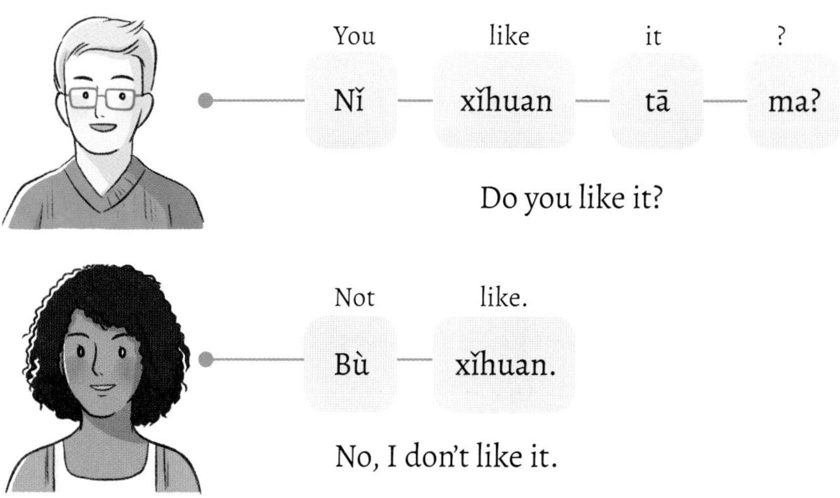

You like it ?
Nǐ xǐhuan tā ma?
Do you like it?
Not like.
Bù xǐhuan.
No, I don't like it.

Comprehension Check

		T	F
1	The Chinese word ma is added to the end of a sentence to form a question.	○	○
2	When turning a statement into a question in Chinese, the word order changes.	○	○
3	For basic sentences, Chinese word order is the same as English word order.	○	○

Useful phrases for the classroom

Here are some important phrases that might come up during class.

Lǎoshī hǎo!

Hello and Goodbye

Audio

1 Nǐ hǎo! — Hello! (Literally: You good)

2 Lǎoshī hǎo! — Hello, Teacher! (Literally: Teacher good)

3 Zàijiàn! — Goodbye! (Literally: Again see)

Knowledge and Understanding

Here are two questions your teacher may ask to check your understanding.

Audio

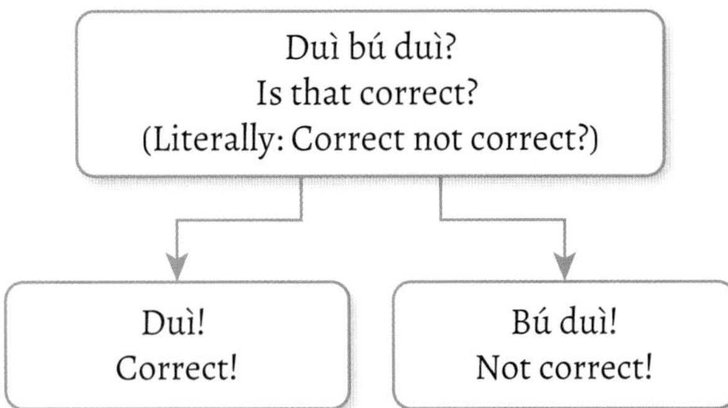

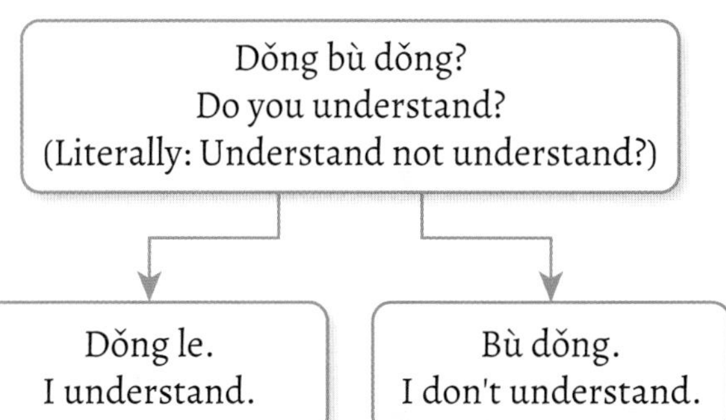

TAKE NOTE

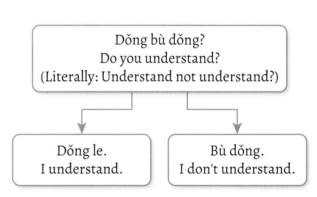

Some of the questions above have the word **bù** (not) in them. The pattern verb + **bù** + verb is another way to ask a question. Although **bù** is typically a fourth tone syllable, it is usually pronounced with a second tone (as **bú**) when it appears directly in front of another fourth tone syllable.

Audio

Here are some additional Chinese phrases that are useful if you want to learn more or don't know the answer to a question.

1 "..." yòng Zhōngwén zěnme shuō? — How do you say "..." in Chinese?

2 Wǒ bù zhīdào. — I don't know.

Being Polite

In the classroom and beyond, being polite helps lead to more successful interactions with other people. Here are a few polite phrases in Mandarin:

Audio

1. Xièxie! — Thank you!
2. Duìbuqǐ! — I'm sorry!; Excuse me!
3. Méi guānxi! — It's nothing!; That's all right! (a common response to "I'm sorry")

Making Requests

It is important to understand requests that your teacher may make of you. A simple way to identify a request is to listen for the word **qǐng**, which is similar to the English word "please." When placed in front of a command, **qǐng** softens the request to make it more polite.

Here are some requests your teacher might make:

Audio

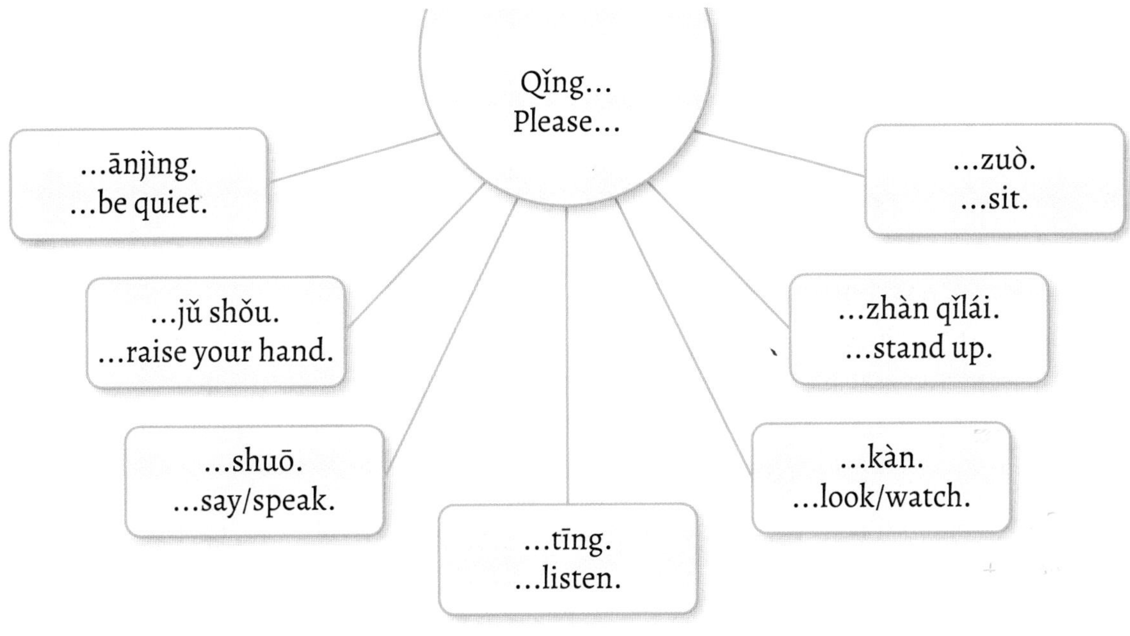

Comprehension Check

	T	F
1 The word **bù** is always pronounced as a fourth tone.	○	○
2 The word **xièxie** means "thank you."	○	○
3 The word **qǐng** is often used when making requests.	○	○

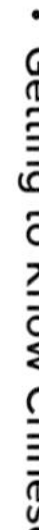

Writing characters is as easy as one, two, three...

Chinese characters are written using a series of lines called "strokes." Characters were traditionally written using ink and a brush so a stroke was a line that could be written without lifting up the brush.

Just as you were probably taught to start at the top when you write the letter "a," Chinese students are taught a specific way to write each character. In general, characters are written from left to right, from top to bottom, and from outside to inside. There are some exceptions, but these basic guidelines are a starting point to learning to write Chinese characters.

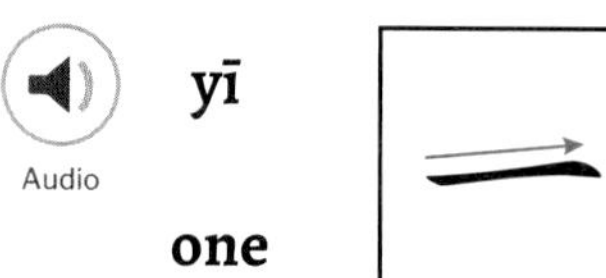

Horizontal strokes in Chinese characters are written from left to right, as shown above.

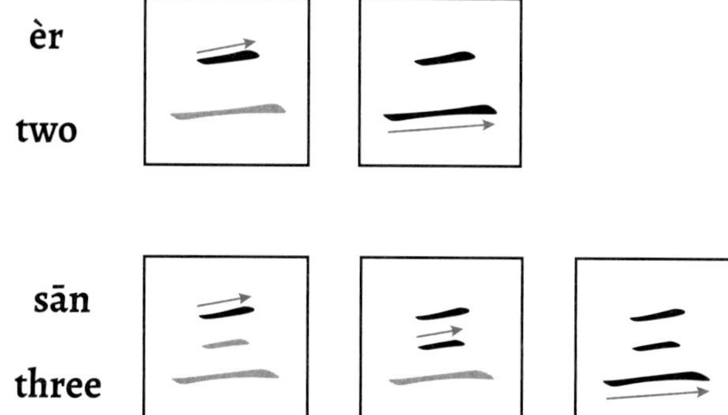

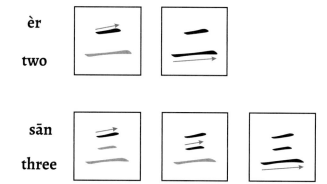

When there are multiple strokes, the upper strokes are written before the bottom stroke.

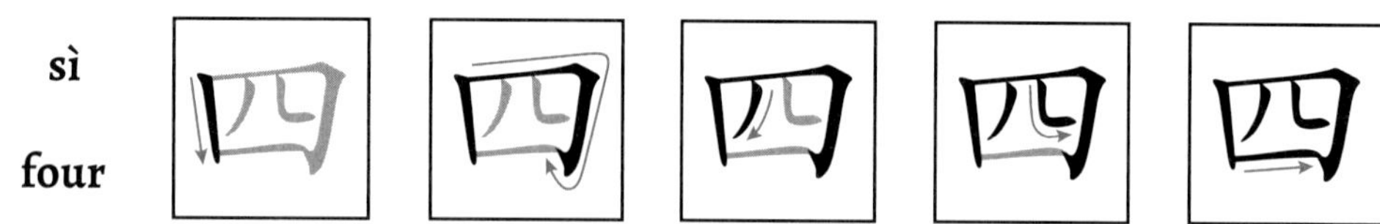

Some Chinese characters, such as 四, include a box-like portion. When writing characters that include this box-like portion, begin with the left side of the box. Then, the top and right sides are added as a single stroke. Next, write the strokes on the inside. Finish the character by adding the bottom stroke to close the box.

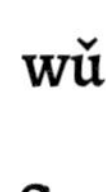

wǔ

five

liù

six

qī

seven

 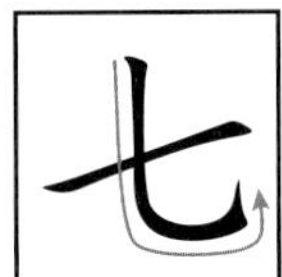

bā

eight

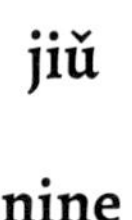

jiǔ

nine

 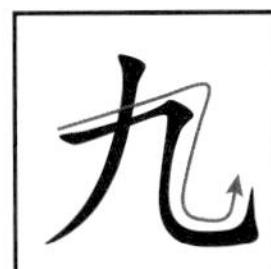 

shí

ten

 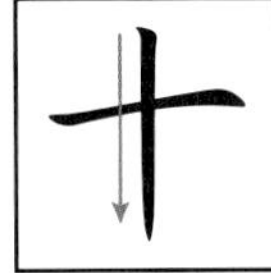

Comprehension Check

		T	F
1	Traditionally, Chinese people wrote with pen and ink.	○	○
2	Chinese characters are usually written from bottom to top.	○	○
3	In the character 四 the top and right sides of the box are written with a single stroke.	○	○

Writing more complex characters and sentences

As you begin to read Chinese, you will notice that most Chinese characters are more complicated than the characters for the numbers one through ten. In addition, it takes time to get used to the different spacing and punctuation used in Chinese sentences.

Sentences

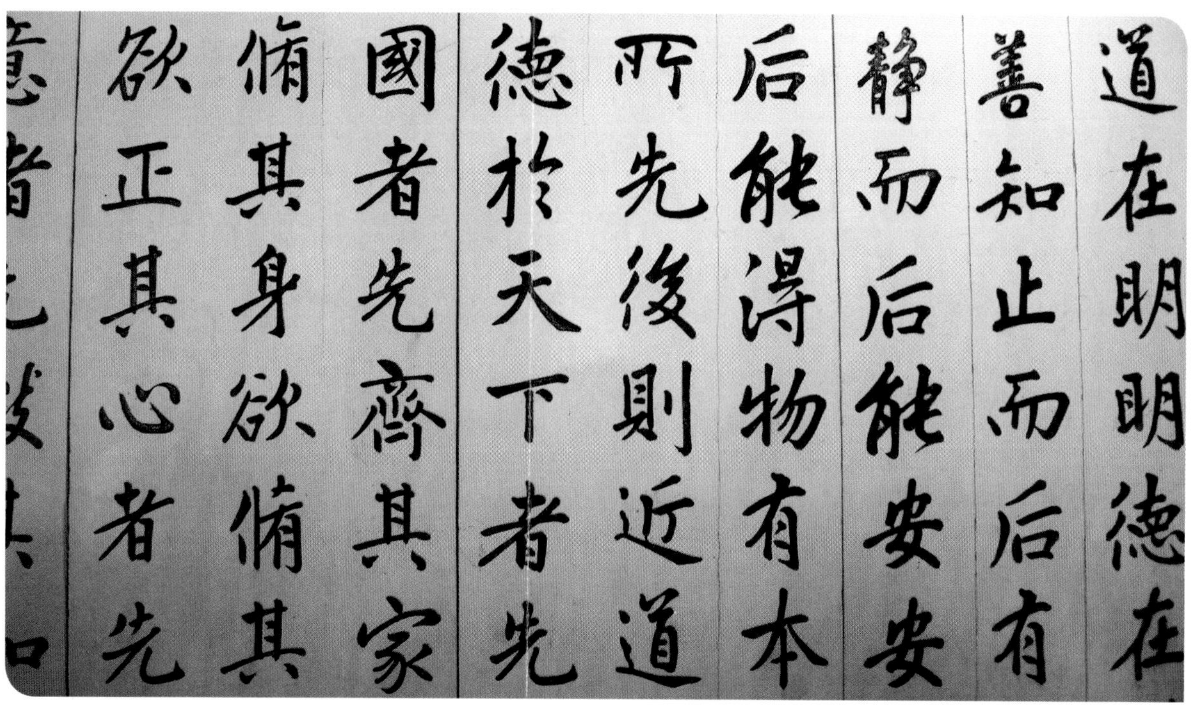

Although Chinese sentences were once written in vertical columns from right to left, they are now typically written horizontally from left to right. In Chinese sentences there are no spaces between words. This may seem challenging at first, but the pinyin support offered in this textbook can help make the separation between words more clear.

On the next page you will find two brief exchanges. Refer to the pinyin on the right as well as the vocabulary list below for help reading the sentences. You will notice that it is not possible to make a word-for-word translation from Chinese to English. Some words that appear in English sentences, including "a" and "the," do not appear in Chinese sentences.

Audio

你好！你是老师吗？ Nǐ hǎo! Nǐ shì lǎoshī ma?

我不是老师，我是学生。 Wǒ bú shì lǎoshī, wǒ shì xuéshēng.

....

再见！ Zàijiàn!

再见！ Zàijiàn!

Vocabulary

Audio

	Word	Pinyin	Meaning
1	你好	nǐ hǎo	hello
2	你	nǐ	you
3	好	hǎo	fine, good, nice; OK, it's settled
4	是	shì	to be
5	老师	lǎoshī	teacher
6	吗	ma	(question word)
7	我	wǒ	I, me
8	不	bù	no, not
9	学生	xuéshēng	student
10	再见	zàijiàn	goodbye, see you again

Character Components

Most Chinese characters are made up of multiple components. Characters with multiple components may seem very complicated, since they have more strokes, but they are still written in the same basic order that you learned earlier: left to right, top to bottom, outside to inside.

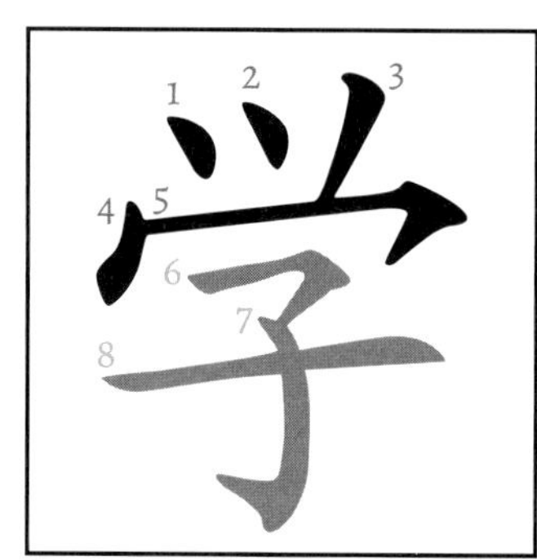

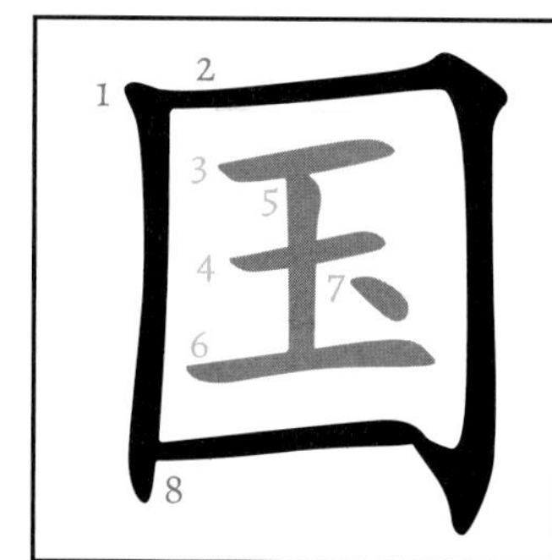

The word 好 is made up of two components, one on the left and one on the right. When writing 好 and most other left-right characters, write the left-hand component before the right-hand component. Similarly, for a top-bottom character like 学 the top component should typically be written before the bottom component. And for enclosing characters like the character for "country," 国 (guó), the outside component (except for the bottom stroke of the box) is written before the inside component.

As you learn more characters, you will see certain components again and again. Once you can recognize some common character components, it will become easier to learn new characters because you will see that even very complex characters are made up of simpler components. As you go through this book, the **What a Character!** feature in each chapter will teach you the meanings of some common components.

Comprehension Check

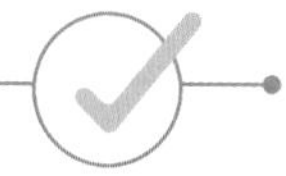

		T	F
1	Today, Chinese sentences are usually written in horizontal lines, from left to right.	○	○
2	For an enclosing Chinese character, the inside component should be finished before beginning to write the outside component.	○	○

CHAPTER 1

Put the Pieces Together!

A Reading and Listening INTERPRETIVE

Passage 1 Look at the Chinese signs below. What numbers can you find on the signs?

A

A sign on a busy road in Beijing

B

A street sign in Shanghai

C

A street sign in Chengdu

D

A tourist sign for a street in the ancient town of Qibao

Passage 2 Are the following math equations correct or incorrect?

		Correct	Incorrect
1	一 + 四 = 六	○	○
2	九 − 八 = 一	○	○
3	三 + 五 = 八	○	○
4	十 − 二 = 七	○	○

Passage 3 Read the dialogue. Are the statements that follow true (T) or false (F)?

Person A 你好！

Person B 你好！ 你是学生吗？

Person A 我不是学生。我是老师。

Comprehension Check

		T	F
1	Person B asks if Person A is a teacher.	○	○
2	Person A is a teacher.	○	○

Audio

Passage 4 Listen to the recording and select the image that best matches the meaning of each sentence.

A

B

C

B Speaking INTERPERSONAL

Here are some access code numbers written in Chinese characters. With a partner, take turns reading the numbers in English and then in Mandarin.

1	七九九	七一九	一三四
2	三六一	三六二	九八一
3	七五八	六一八	四一六
4	八一五	九四一	二二八
5	四一二	九八六	八一六
6	八三八	一三六	一二四

C Final Project

Practice Chinese numbers by playing a simple card game.

Step 1: Cut a sheet of paper into ten equal pieces. Number each piece from one to ten in Chinese characters. You now have a set of Chinese number cards.

Step 2: Shuffle your cards and hold them face down.

Step 3: Pair up with another student who has finished making his or her set of number cards. Flip over the top card in each of your decks at the same time. Subtract the smaller number from the larger number on the two cards and quickly give the answer in Chinese. Whoever gives the correct answer first wins a point.

Note: If you and your partner turn the same number over at the same time, the correct answer will be 零 (líng), which means "zero."

Learning Habits

Active participation in class is essential to learning Chinese. Each week, take a moment to think about whether or not you:

- Came to class prepared
- Listened attentively
- Tried to focus when your mind wandered
- Tried to speak in Chinese
- Asked questions when confused

Can-Do Goals

Talk with your teacher if you are not certain you understand:

- Something about different Chinese dialects
- What a Chinese character is
- How to read pinyin
- The structure of simple Chinese sentences

Before you start Chapter 2, make sure you can:

- Greet someone in Chinese
- Say some simple sentences in Chinese
- Understand some words and phrases for the classroom
- Write the numbers one through ten in Chinese

Cultural Knowledge

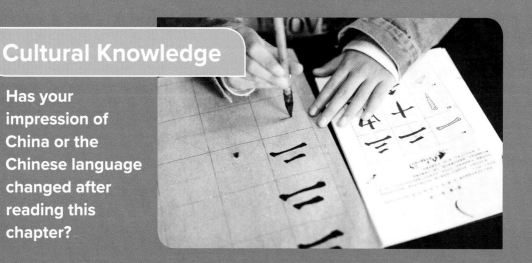

Has your impression of China or the Chinese language changed after reading this chapter?

What's in a Name?

CHAPTER 2

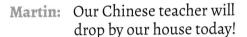

第 dì 二 èr 课 kè

Martin: Our Chinese teacher will drop by our house today!

Isabella: Really? So he speaks English, right?

Martin: I guess so. But I can't wait to practice Chinese with him!

Isabella: I want to make a good first impression! Why don't we practice before we meet with him?

Martin: Sure!

Can-Do Goals

In this chapter, you will learn to:

- Understand how Chinese names are different from English names
- Tell others your name
- Ask for someone's name
- Say that something belongs to someone
- Respond to "what" and "who" questions
- Express that you have or do not have something

CULTURE CONNECTION

míngzi

名字

Names

Chinese names are usually made up of two to three characters: a one-character family name followed by a one- or two-character given name. Names are important! They make an impression on others, and some Chinese people believe that a person's name can affect his or her future. Instead of picking from a list of given names, Chinese parents will combine almost any characters in the language to create meaningful and unique names for their children.

Isabella's Chinese name is 林春月 (Lín Chūnyuè). She picked 春 (spring) for her favorite season and 月 (moon) because she is a night owl. She and Martin chose the family name 林 together in Chinese class. In China, children usually inherit their father's family name. Their mother might have a different family name since Chinese women generally do not change their names after marriage.

Martin's Chinese name is 林马丁 (Lín Mădīng), which he chose because it sounds similar to his English name. This is typically how Chinese names are assigned to non-Chinese public figures. For example, the American author Mark Twain is called Măkè Tŭwēn.

By the Numbers

Even though there are more people in China than in any other country, eighty-five percent of the Chinese population has one of the 100 most common surnames. All together, more than 260,000,000 Chinese people have the surnames 李 (Lǐ), 王 (Wáng), and 张 (Zhāng). Here are these three surnames written in ink with a brush:

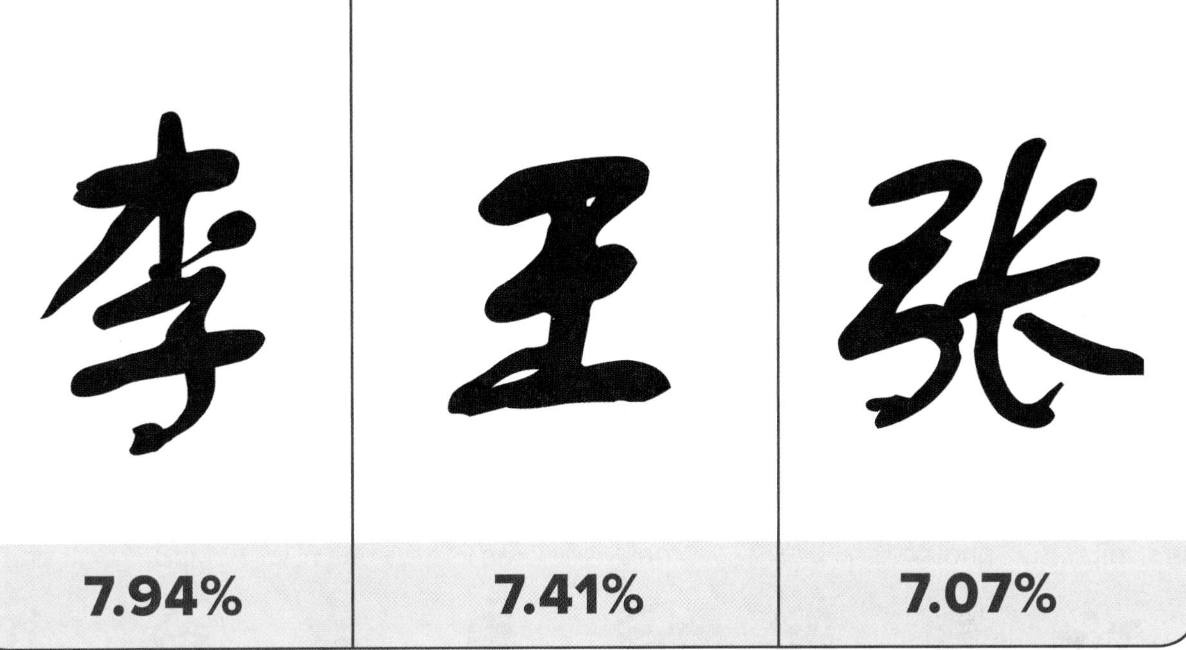

Source: Population Census Office of the State Council of the People's Republic of China, 2010

REFLECT ON THE ESSENTIAL QUESTION

How do we form first impressions?

1. Does your name give people an impression of what you are like?
2. If you could easily change your name, would you? Why or why not?
3. Do you have a Chinese name? If so, how was it chosen?

Exchanging names

1a Language Model TARGET LANGUAGE INPUT

Your teacher will lead a discussion about the image below. Try to participate as much as you can. If there is anything you don't understand, let your teacher know.

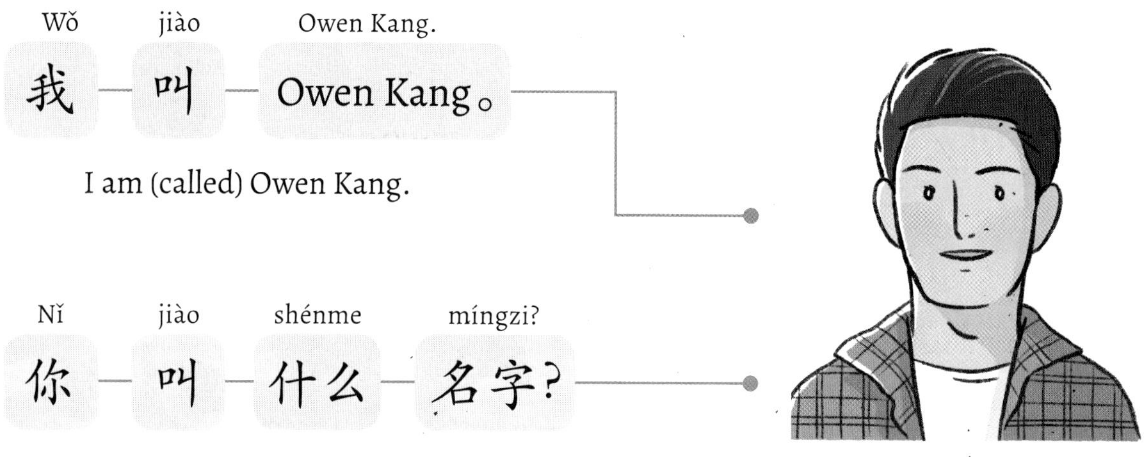
Wǒ jiào Owen Kang.
我 叫 Owen Kang。
I am (called) Owen Kang.
Nǐ jiào shénme míngzi?
你 叫 什么 名字?
What is your name?

Alex?
Taylor?
Jordan?
Sam?
Jesse?

1b New Words in Conversation INTERPRETIVE

Listen to the audio and try to understand as much as you can of the phone conversation between Daming and his new student. Then read the dialogue, using the pinyin text and vocabulary list to figure out unfamiliar words.

你好！我叫 Owen Kang。你叫什么名字？

Nǐ hǎo! Wǒ jiào Owen Kang. Nǐ jiào shénme míngzi?

你好！ 我的英文名字是 Dan Bai。 我的中文名字是白大明。你的中文名字是什么？

Nǐ hǎo! Wǒ de Yīngwén míngzi shì Dan Bai. Wǒ de Zhōngwén míngzi shì Bái Dàmíng. Nǐ de Zhōngwén míngzi shì shénme?

我的中文名字是大文。

Wǒ de Zhōngwén míngzi shì Dàwén.

Comprehension Check

		T	F
1	Owen tells Daming his name.	○	○
2	Daming does not have an English name.	○	○
3	Owen's Chinese name is Dàwén.	○	○

Vocabulary

	Word	Pinyin	Meaning
1	叫	jiào	to be called
2	什么	shénme	what
3	名字	míngzi	name
4	的	de	(a possessive word that shows that something belongs to somebody)
5	英文	Yīngwén	English (language)
6	中文	Zhōngwén	Chinese (language)
	白大明	Bái Dàmíng	Daming Bai (a person's name)

1c Puzzle It Out PROGRESS CHECK

Complete the exercise below to check your understanding of what you learned in Section 1. If you have questions, consult the Language Reference section.

Rearrange the Chinese words in each row to translate the English phrases.

1 我 | 老师 | 的
my teacher

2 名字 | 的 | 老师
the teacher's name

3 是 | 你 | 什么？| 的 | 中文 | 名字
What's your Chinese name?

Language Reference

1 Indicating possession with 的

Adding 的 (de) between two nouns shows that the second person or thing belongs to the first.

	Noun 1	的	Noun 2	Meaning
1	我	de 的	老师	my teacher
2	Bái 白老师	de 的	学生	Mr. Bai's students
3	学生	de 的	Yīngwén míngzi 英文名字	the student's English name

2 Using question words such as 什么

When asking a question in Chinese, the order of the words in the sentence does not change, even when using question words such as 什么 (shénme).

1 A: 你叫什么名字? (jiào shénme míngzi) — What is your name? (Literally: What name are you called?)

B: 我叫白大明。 (jiào Bái Dàmíng) — My name is Daming Bai. (Literally: I am called Daming Bai.)

2 A: 你的英文名字是什么? (de Yīngwén míngzi shénme) — What is your English name?

B: 我的英文名字是 Sarah。 (de Yīngwén míngzi) — My English name is Sarah.

In both China and the United States, students usually do not use their teachers' given names. In English, we address teachers as "Mr." or "Ms.," but in Chinese teachers are addressed as 老师. Since Daming is Owen's new tutor, Owen might call him 白老师 to be extra formal and polite.

1d Using the Language INTERPERSONAL

Activity 1 Find out your classmates' Chinese and English names. Use the questions below as a guide.

- 你的英文名字是什么？
- 你的中文名字是什么？

Activity 2 The pinyin of several famous people's Chinese names are below. What do you think their English names are? Write down the English names, then compare notes with a partner. (Hint: The Chinese names sound like the English names.)

Example: A 的英文名字是什么？

A

Àisàkè Niúdùn

Famous English mathematician and scientist

B

Mǎdīng Lùdé Jīn

Famous American activist

C

Ānnī Fǎlánkè

Famous for her diary, which was published after her death

D

Àopǔlā Wēnfúruì

Famous American television host

Saying that you have (or don't have) something

2a Language Model TARGET LANGUAGE INPUT

Your teacher will lead a discussion about the images below. Try to participate as much as you can. If there is anything you don't understand, let your teacher know.

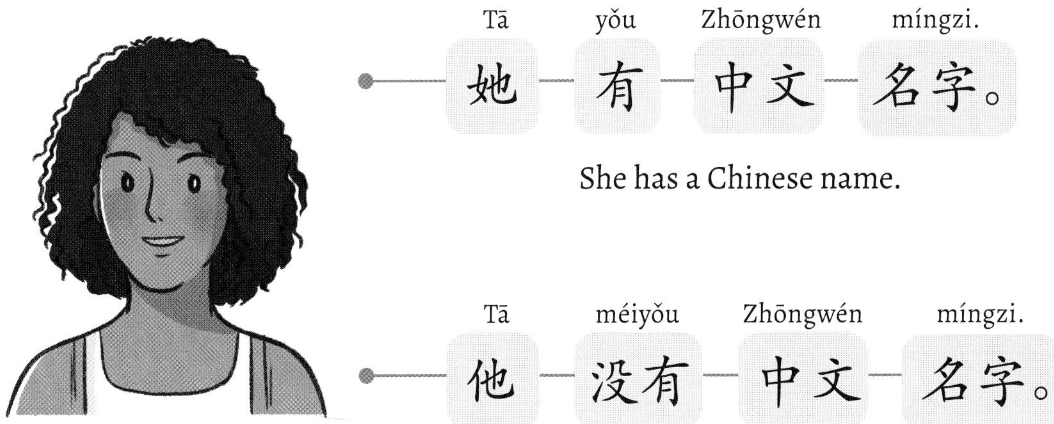
Tā yǒu Zhōngwén míngzi.
她 有 中文 名字。

She has a Chinese name.

Tā méiyǒu Zhōngwén míngzi.
他 没有 中文 名字。

He does not have a Chinese name.

李月

Chris

Audio

2b New Words in Conversation INTERPRETIVE

Listen to the audio and try to understand as much as you can. Then read the dialogue, using the pinyin text and vocabulary list to figure out unfamiliar words.

春月，她是谁？她是你的老师吗？

Chūnyuè, tā shì shéi? Tā shì nǐ de lǎoshī ma?

她不是我的老师，马丁。她是我的同学。

Tā bú shì wǒ de lǎoshī, Mǎdīng. Tā shì wǒ de tóngxué.

她叫什么名字？

Tā jiào shénme míngzi?

她叫 Abby。

Tā jiào Abby.

她有中文名字吗？

Tā yǒu Zhōngwén míngzi ma?

她没有中文名字。

Tā méiyǒu Zhōngwén míngzi.

Comprehension Check

		T	F
1	Martin and Isabella are talking about Isabella's teacher.	○	○
2	Martin asks what Isabella's Chinese name is.	○	○
3	Abby has an English name, but not a Chinese name.	○	○

Vocabulary

Audio

	Word	Pinyin	Meaning
7	她	tā	she, her
8	谁	shéi	who
9	同学	tóngxué	classmate
10	有	yǒu	to have
11	没有	méiyǒu	to not have
12	他	tā	he, him
	林春月	Lín Chūnyuè	Isabella Lopez (a person's name)
	林马丁	Lín Mădīng	Martin Lopez (a person's name)

2c Puzzle It Out PROGRESS CHECK

Complete the exercise below to check your understanding of what you learned in Section 2. If you have questions, consult the Language Reference section.

Use the words in the list to complete the translation of the dialogue below.

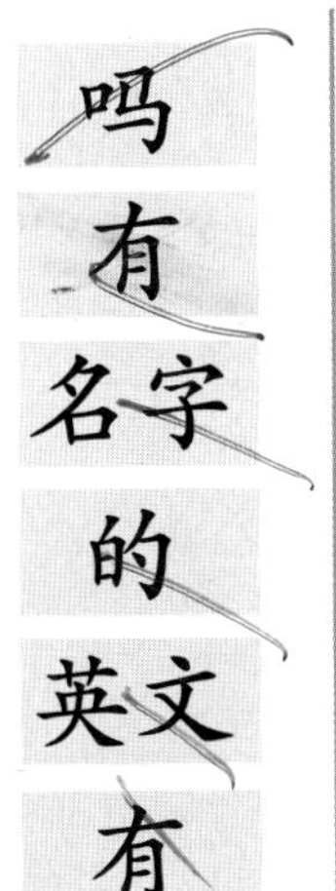

A: 你 ______ ______ 名字 ______ ?

Do you have an English name?

B: ______ ，我 ______ 英文 ______ 是 Sarita。

I do. My English name is Sarita.

3 Expressing having and not having with 有 and 没有

有 (yǒu) is different from other Chinese verbs because the word 没 (méi) is used for the negative form instead of 不 .

Q: 你有 (yǒu) 中文名字吗？ — Do you have a Chinese name?

A1: 我有 (yǒu) 中文名字。 — I have a Chinese name.

A2: 我没有 (méiyǒu) 中文名字。 — I do not have a Chinese name.

Questions with 有 (yǒu) can also be answered more simply by just responding 有 (yǒu) or 没有 (méiyǒu).

Q: 你有 (yǒu) 英文名字吗？ — Do you have an English name?

A: 有 (yǒu)。/ 没有 (méiyǒu)。 — Yes, I do. / No, I don't.

You know how to say two of the 5W's, "who" and "what," in Chinese. Ask your teacher how to say the remaining W's. Refer back to Topic 4 in Chapter 1 if you need a reminder of how to use Chinese to ask for the Chinese word for something.

2d Using the Language INTERPERSONAL

Your class is shopping for some school supplies from Taobao, China's largest online shopping website. Working in small groups, use the words given in the image to ask your groupmates whether they have certain items.

Ask your classmates: 你有 _____ 吗？

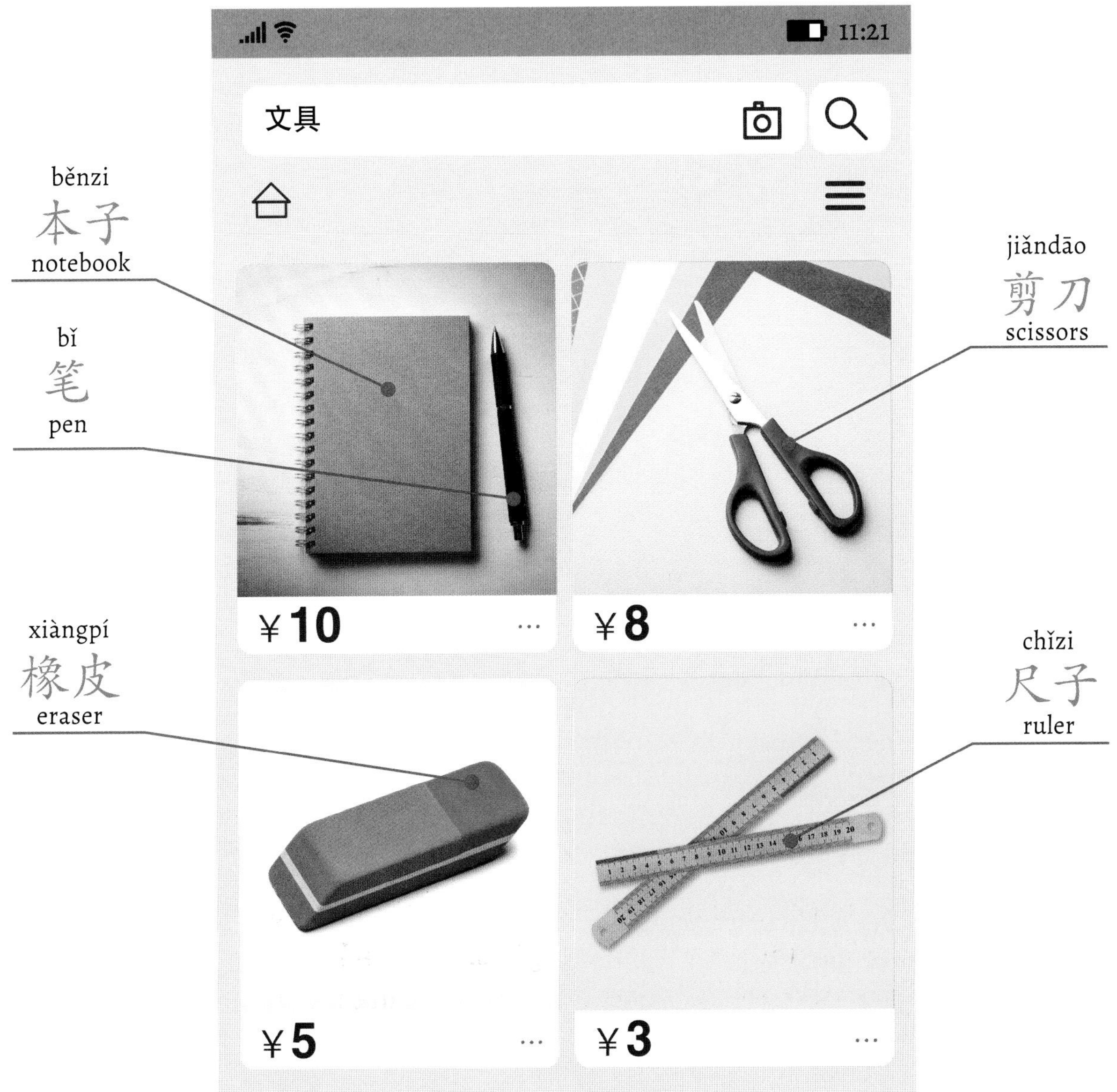

Introducing more than one person

3a Language Model TARGET LANGUAGE INPUT

Your teacher will lead a discussion about the images below. Try to participate as much as you can. If there is anything you don't understand, let your teacher know.

Tāmen shì xuéshēng.
他们 — 是 — 学生。

They are students.

Nǐmen yě shì xuéshēng ma?
你们 — 也 — 是 — 学生 — 吗？

Are you (plural) also students?

1 tāmen
他们
they, them (if anyone in the group is male)

2 tāmen
她们
they, them (if everyone in the group is female)

3 wǒmen
我们
we, us

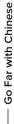

3b New Words in Conversation INTERPRETIVE

Listen to the audio and try to understand as much as you can. Then read the dialogue, using the pinyin text and vocabulary list to figure out unfamiliar words.

他们是谁? — Tāmen shì shéi?

他们是我和 Leo 的同学。 — Tāmen shì wǒ hé Leo de tóngxué.

她们也是你们的同学吗? — Tāmen yě shì nǐmen de tóngxué ma?

不是，她们是我们的朋友。 — Bú shì, tāmen shì wǒmen de péngyou.

Comprehension Check

		T	F
1	The people in the first group are Leo and Maya's classmates.	○	○
2	The people in the second group are also Leo and Maya's classmates.	○	○
3	The second group of people includes a mix of boys and girls.	○	○

Vocabulary

	Word	Pinyin	Meaning
13	他们	tāmen	they, them (if anyone in the group is male)
14	和	hé	and
15	她们	tāmen	they, them (if everyone in the group is female)
16	也	yě	also, too, as well as
17	你们 	nǐmen	you (plural)
18	我们	wǒmen	we, us
19	朋友 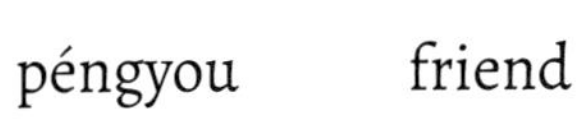	péngyou	friend

Chapter 2 • What's in a Name? • Section 3

3c Puzzle It Out PROGRESS CHECK

Complete the exercise below to check your understanding of what you learned in Section 3. If you have questions, consult the Language Reference section.

Rearrange the Chinese words in each row to translate the English sentences.

1 他 | 的 | 同学 | 是 | 吗？| 你们 | 她 | 和

Are she and he your classmates?

2 也 | 我们 | 他们 | 朋友。| 是 | 的

We are also their friends.

Language Reference

4 Using the connecting words 和 and 也

Like the English word "and," 和 (hé) can connect nouns. However, 和 (hé) cannot be used to connect two sentences.

1 我和(hé)他是林老师的学生。 He and I are Ms. Lin's students.

也 (yě) means "also" or "as well as." 也 (yě) typically comes after the subject of the sentence (shown in bold below) and before the verb. It cannot come at the end of a sentence.

2 我是林老师的学生。

他也(yě)是林老师的学生。

I'm Ms. Lin's student.
He's also Ms. Lin's student.

3 马丁不是我的同学。

春月也(yě)不是我的同学。

Martin is not my classmate. Isabella is also not my classmate.

Two sentences with the same subject can be combined using 也 (yě) and then the subject is not repeated.

4	我是你的老师。我也(yě)是你的朋友(péngyou)。	I am your teacher. I am also your friend.
	→ 我是你的老师，也(yě)是你的朋友(péngyou)。	I am your teacher as well as your friend.

3d Using the Language INTERPERSONAL

Activity 1 In pairs, say as much as you can about the people in the images below. Use 也 to describe what these people have in common.

Example:

Isabella 有中文名字。Martin 也有中文名字。

Isabella

春月

Martin

马丁

Dan Bai

白大明

Activity 2 Do you and the students in your group have the same teachers?

Step 1: Using the example below as a guide, interview the other students and keep track of their responses.

Example:

Henderson 老师是我的老师。她也是你们的老师吗?

Step 2: Using your notes, tell the rest of the class which of your teachers are shared by other students in your group.

Example:

Henderson 老师是我的老师。她也是 Nico, Bryan 和 Elisa 的老师。

This component is derived from the character 人 (rén), which means "person." The component 亻 (rén) mostly appears on the left side of characters. The meaning of characters with this component sometimes relates to "person" or "people."

Which characters below have the 亻 (rén) component?

1 你 2 也 3 他 4 我 5 没
6 什 7 们 8 中 9 谁 10 林

Put the Pieces Together!

A Reading and Listening INTERPRETIVE

Passage 1

MARTIN AND ISABELLA MEET THEIR CHINESE TUTOR, DAMING BAI, FOR THE FIRST TIME.

6
白老师，我也有中文名字。我的中文名字是春月。
You guys don't have to call me 白老师. Just call me 大明.
7
8
你好， Ms. Lopez.
你好，大明！
I'm afraid my Chinese is not as good as Martin's or Isabella's!
9
I love learning Chinese. I can't wait to get to Beijing!
10
What about you, Isabella?
I don't know... I feel like Martin is better at learning languages than me.
Don't worry-- anyone can learn a language. You learned English when you were a baby, right?

Comprehension Check

		T	F
1	Martin and Isabella greet Daming as 白老师.	○	○
2	Isabella does not use her English name when introducing herself.	○	○
3	Daming asks them to call him by his English name.	○	○

Passage 2 Read the conversation between two new students. Are the statements that follow true (T) or false (F)?

First new student:	你好！我叫明明。我是学生。 你也是学生吗？
Second new student:	我也是学生。你的老师是谁？
First new student:	我的老师是白老师。
Second new student:	白老师也是我的老师！我们是同学。

		T	F
1	The first new student's name is Mingming.	○	○
2	The first student says that he likes his teacher.	○	○
3	These students learn that they are classmates.	○	○

Passage 3 For thousands of years, ink seals were used as official signatures. People still make traditional name seals today, but they are often used for personal enjoyment or as an artistic signature. Can you tell to whom these seals belong? (Hint: Remember that in the past Chinese was not written from left to right.)

1

2

3

4

Passage 4 Listen to the recording and answer the following questions. Select all that apply.

1 The speaker says he

(a) has an English name.
(b) studies English.
(c) has a Chinese name.

2 The speaker asks if

(a) you are all classmates.
(b) you all have Chinese names.
(c) you all have English names.

Passage 5 Listen to the recording and select the image that best matches the meaning of each sentence.

A

B

C

D

B Speaking INTERPERSONAL

Refer to the chart and ask your partner which school supplies these students have or do not have. Follow the model below.

Example:

A: Ellen 有笔(bǐ)吗?

B: 她有笔(bǐ)。 Miko 也有笔(bǐ)。

	 Ellen	 Miko	 Leo	 Sanjay
 bǐ	✓	✓	✓	✓
 běnzi	✗	✓	✓	✗
 chǐzi	✗	✓	✗	✗
 xiàngpí	✓	✗	✓	✓
 jiǎndāo	✗	✗	✗	✗

C Final Project PRESENTATIONAL

Self-Introduction Poster

A group of exchange students from Beijing is going to join your Chinese class soon. Your teacher has asked each person in the class to create a self-introduction poster to help the exchange students get to know your class. Refer to Isabella's poster as an example and make one for yourself.

Step 1: Take note of the information included on Isabella's introduction poster.

Step 2: Create a poster about yourself and, if you want, include your picture.

Step 3: Write your Chinese name on the poster and illustrate its meaning using pictures or symbols.

Step 4: Present your poster to the class and introduce yourself.

Can-Do Goals

Talk with your teacher if you have questions or if you are not certain you can do the following tasks:

- Understand how Chinese names are different from English names
- Tell others your name
- Ask for someone's name
- Say that something belongs to someone
- Respond to "what" and "who" questions
- Express that you have or do not have something

Cultural Knowledge

What did you learn about Chinese names?

Tell Me About Yourself

CHAPTER 3

第 dì

课 kè

Isabella, Martin, and Daming are gathered in the Lopezes' dining room. The conversation turns to Daming's family in China.

Isabella: Your family must miss you when you're here in the U.S.

Daming: Yes, and I miss them, too, sometimes.

Martin: Do you have any brothers or sisters?

Daming: I'll tell you more, but we need to stick to speaking in Chinese!

Can-Do Goals

In this chapter, you will learn to:

- Understand simple descriptions of families
- Ask and answer questions about family members
- Express how many siblings and pets you have
- Understand when others talk about their likes and dislikes
- Talk about likes and dislikes
- Use different measure words to talk about people and animals

CULTURE CONNECTION

jiātíng

家庭

Family

The saying 三代同堂 (sān dài tóng táng), which means "three generations under one roof," gives an impression of traditional family life in China. Imagine children, parents, and grandparents living together and caring for each other. Families in China are changing, but many values, such as a close relationship between generations, are still important.

Respect Your Elders

In Chinese culture, it is important to show respect for those who are older than you, even among siblings. Older brothers are called 哥哥 (gēge); older sisters are called 姐姐 (jiějie); younger brothers are 弟弟 (dìdi); and younger sisters are 妹妹 (mèimei). Younger siblings often call their older siblings 哥哥 or 姐姐 rather than just using their names. Even between twins, the older child is 哥哥 or 姐姐, and the younger one is 弟弟 or 妹妹!

A Passion for Pets

Many Chinese people embrace their pets as part of their families. Dogs are the most popular choice of pet in China, followed by cats. This woman in Beijing dyed her dog's fur. Other owners might dress their pets up or even refer to them as 宝贝 (bǎobèi), which means "treasure" or "baby."

By the Numbers

For several decades, the average size of Chinese households has been shrinking. The number of 三代同堂 households has decreased, and the Chinese government has worked to limit the country's population growth. The One-Child Policy, in effect from 1979 to 2015, was a part of the government effort to discourage couples from having many children. Now, small families of three or fewer people are common, especially in cities.

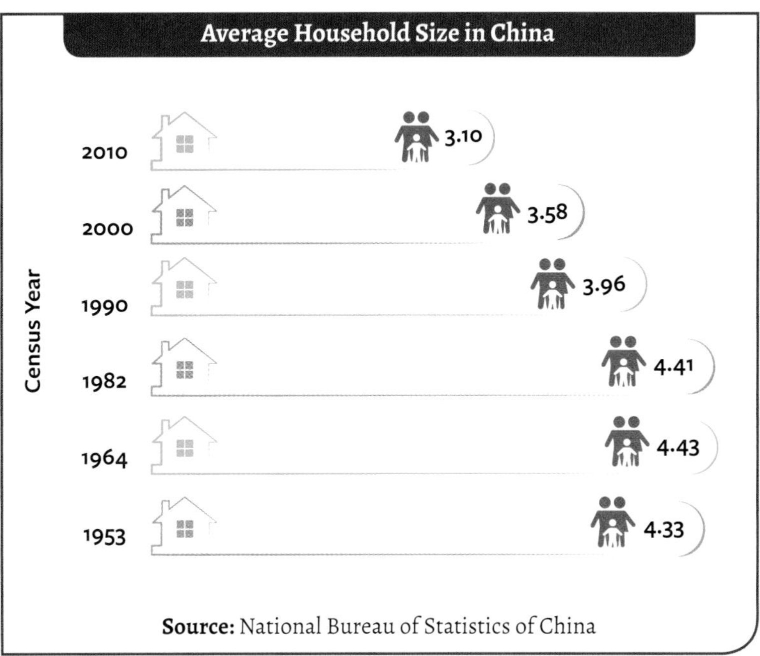

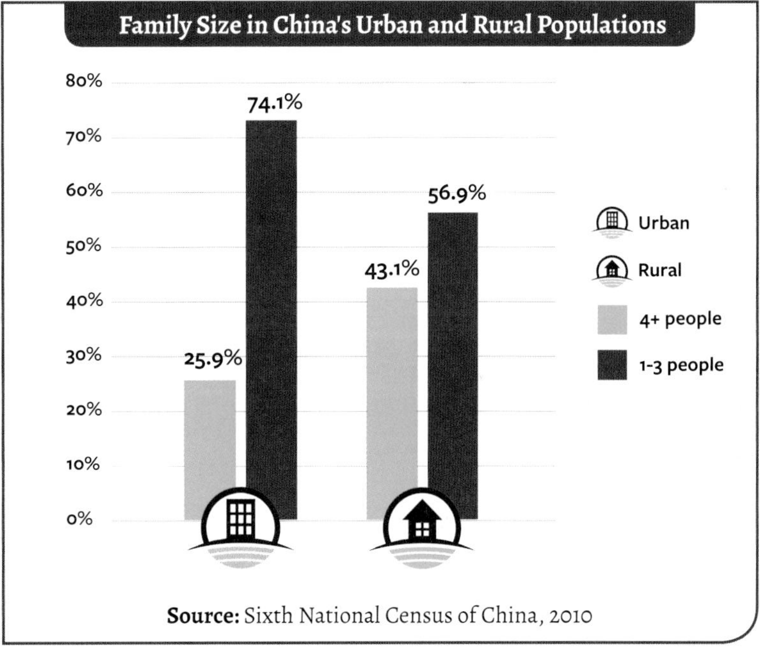

REFLECT ON THE ESSENTIAL QUESTION

How do we form first impressions?

1. What impression do you have of family life in China? How do you think it is similar to or different from family life in your culture?
2. When you know someone is an older or a younger sibling, does it influence your impression of that person?
3. Would you count pets as family members? Why or why not?

Talking about siblings

1a Language Model — TARGET LANGUAGE INPUT

Your teacher will lead a discussion about the family below. Try to participate as much as you can. If there is anything you don't understand, let your teacher know.

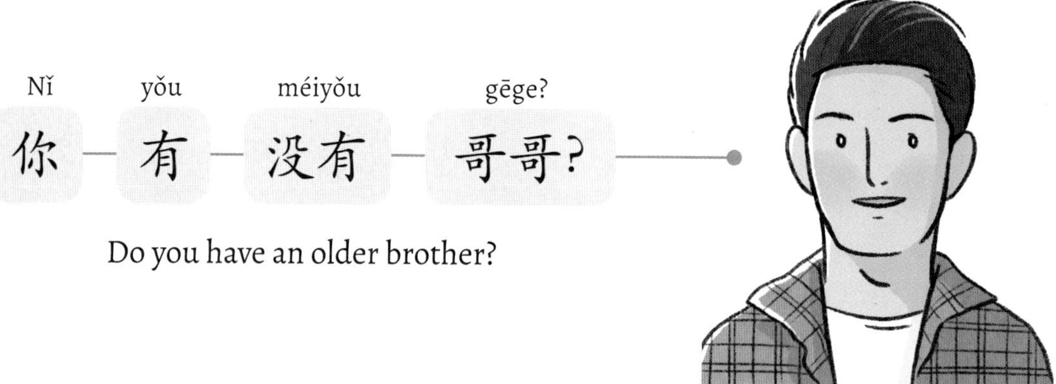

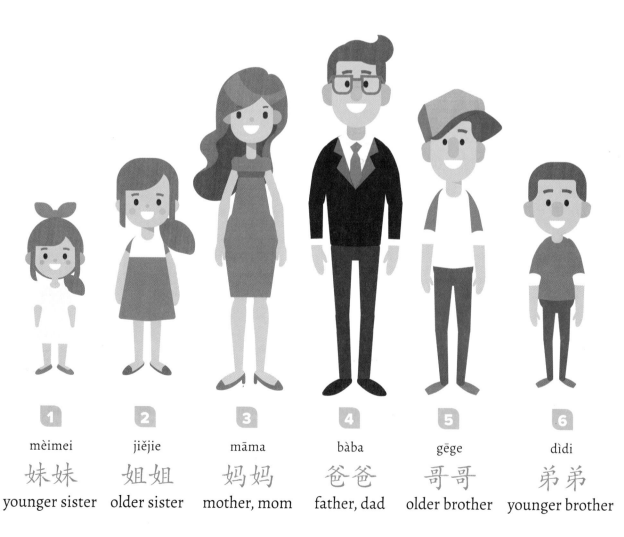

1	2	3	4	5	6
mèimei	jiějie	māma	bàba	gēge	dìdi
妹妹	姐姐	妈妈	爸爸	哥哥	弟弟
younger sister	older sister	mother, mom	father, dad	older brother	younger brother

1b New Words in Conversation INTERPRETIVE

Listen to the audio and try to understand as much as you can. Then read the dialogue, using the pinyin text and vocabulary list to figure out unfamiliar words.

你有没有哥哥？ Nǐ yǒu méiyǒu gēge?

我没有哥哥。我有姐姐。 Wǒ méiyǒu gēge. Wǒ yǒu jiějie.

你有几个姐姐？ Nǐ yǒu jǐ gè jiějie?

我有一个姐姐。 Wǒ yǒu yí gè jiějie.

Comprehension Check

		T	F
1	Ellen has an older brother and an older sister.	○	○
2	Owen asks Ellen how many older sisters she has.	○	○

Vocabulary

Audio

	Word	Pinyin	Meaning
1	哥哥	gēge	older brother
2	姐姐	jiějie	older sister
3	几	jǐ	how many
4	个	gè	(measure word for people and many everyday objects)
5	弟弟	dìdi	younger brother
6	妹妹	mèimei	younger sister
7	爸爸	bàba	father, dad
8	妈妈	māma	mother, mom

1c Puzzle It Out PROGRESS CHECK

Complete the exercises below to check your understanding of what you learned in Section 1. If you have questions, consult the Language Reference section.

Exercise 1 Use the words in the list to complete the translation of the dialogue.

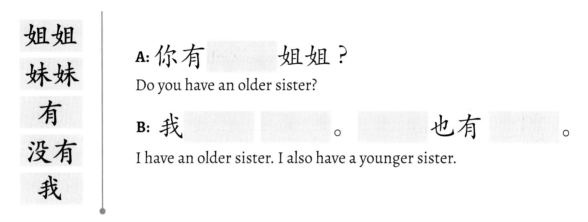

姐姐
妹妹
有
没有
我

A: 你有 ______ 姐姐？
Do you have an older sister?

B: 我 ______ ______。______ 也有 ______。
I have an older sister. I also have a younger sister.

Exercise 2 Should 个 be added to the following sentences? Choose Yes or No.

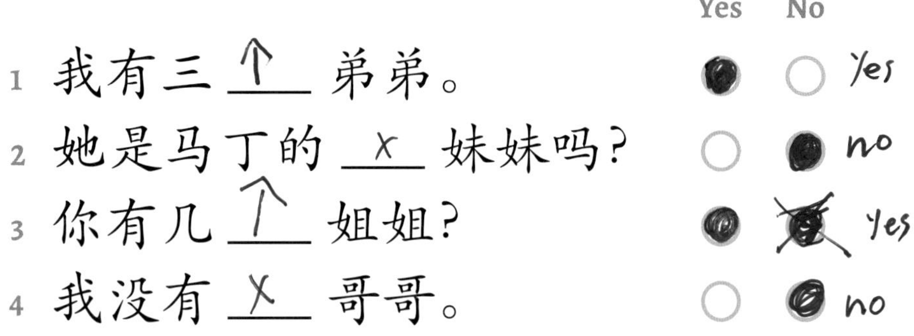

Yes No
1 我有三 ___ 弟弟。
2 她是马丁的 ___ 妹妹吗？
3 你有几 ___ 姐姐？
4 我没有 ___ 哥哥。

Language Reference

1 Using measure words (个)

When counting things in Chinese, a measure word is placed between the number and the thing being counted. English has similar words for describing the amount of something. For example, one can ask for "three *slices* of bread" or "ten *pieces* of paper."

However, in Chinese, there is a measure word for everything! The measure word 个 (gè) is used to count many kinds of things, including people.

gè mèimei

1 我有一个妹妹。 I have one younger sister.

gè

2 老师有十个学生。 The teacher has ten students.

gè

3 五个同学没有中文名字。 Five classmates don't have Chinese names.

TAKE NOTE

There is a special number word used when counting two of something: 两 (liǎng).

liǎng gè gēge

他有两个哥哥。 He has two older brothers.

2 Asking questions using the A不A pattern

Use the A不A pattern to ask yes/no questions. When you use the A不A question pattern, you don't need to use 吗. If the verb is 有, then 没 is used rather than 不.

	A不A		Meaning
Q1 你	是不是	学生?	Are you a student?
Q2 你	有没有	jiějie 姐姐?	Do you have an older sister?

Answer an A不A question the same way you answer a 吗 question.

A1 (是,) 我是学生。 (Yes,) I am a student.

jiějie

A2 (没有,) 我没有姐姐。 (No,) I don't have an older sister.

1d Using the Language INTERPERSONAL

Activity 1 Ask your classmates about their siblings. Use the questions below as a starting point. Does anyone have all four kinds of sibling?

- 你有哥哥吗？
- 你有没有弟弟？

- 你是姐姐吗？
- 你是不是妹妹？

Activity 2 Now that you know who has brothers and sisters, you can find out who has the most brothers and sisters! Ask your classmates how many of each kind of sibling they have.

A: 你有几个妹妹？
B: 我有两个妹妹。

As a character, 女 (nǚ) means "female." When the 女 component appears in a character, the meaning is often related to women.

Daming's friend from Shanghai shared his family tree with Daming. How many female family members does he have?

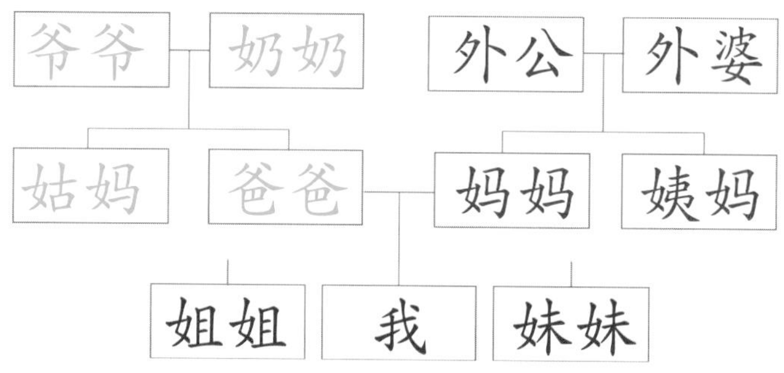

Expressing likes and dislikes

2a Language Model TARGET LANGUAGE INPUT

Your teacher will lead a discussion about the images below. Try to participate as much as you can. If there is anything you don't understand, let your teacher know.

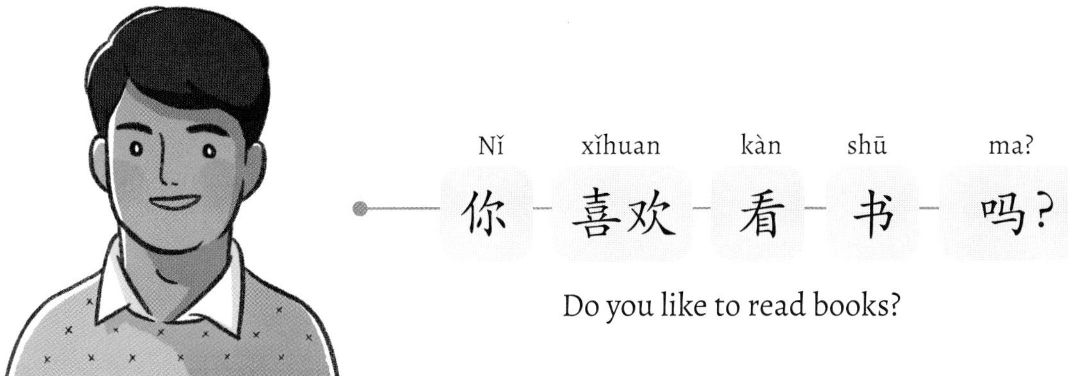

Nǐ xǐhuan kàn shū ma?
你 喜欢 看 书 吗?
Do you like to read books?

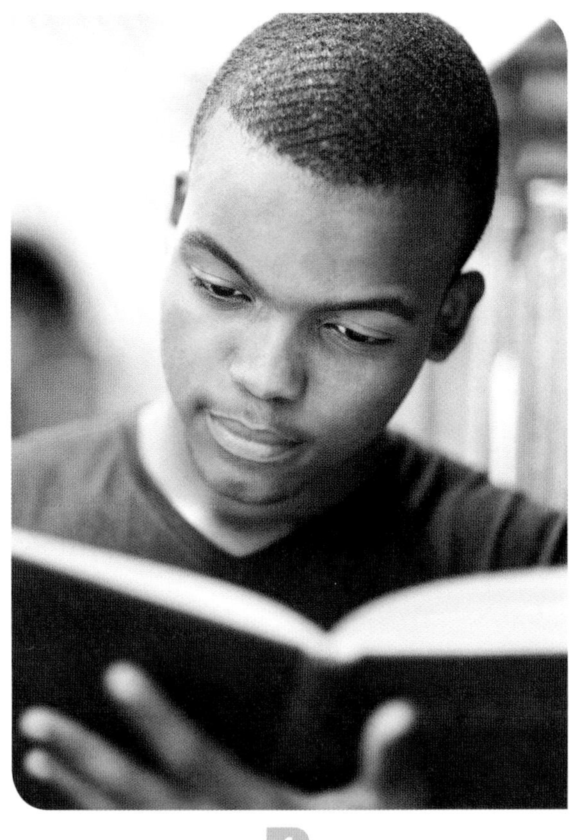

1
kàn shū
看书
to read a book

2
kàn diànshì
看电视
to watch TV

Audio

2b New Words in Conversation INTERPRETIVE

Listen to the audio and try to understand as much as you can. Then read the dialogue, using the pinyin text and vocabulary list to figure out unfamiliar words.

你们喜欢看书吗？ Nǐmen xǐhuan kàn shū ma?

我喜欢看书。我也很喜欢看电视。 Wǒ xǐhuan kàn shū. Wǒ yě hěn xǐhuan kàn diànshì.

我不太喜欢看书，可是我很喜欢看电视。 Wǒ bú tài xǐhuan kàn shū, kěshì wǒ hěn xǐhuan kàn diànshì.

Comprehension Check

		Yes	No	Don't know
1	Does Sanjay like to read?	○	○	○
2	Does Maya like to watch TV?	○	○	○
3	Does Leo like to read?	○	○	○

Audio

Vocabulary

	Word	Pinyin	Meaning
9	喜欢	xǐhuan	to like
10	看	kàn	to look at, to watch, to read, to see
11	书	shū	book
12	很	hěn	very, really
13	电视	diànshì	television
14	不太	bú tài	not really, not very
15	可是	kěshì	but

2c Puzzle It Out PROGRESS CHECK

Complete the exercise below to check your understanding of what you learned in Section 2. If you have questions, consult the Language Reference section.

Make correct sentences by rearranging the words in each row.

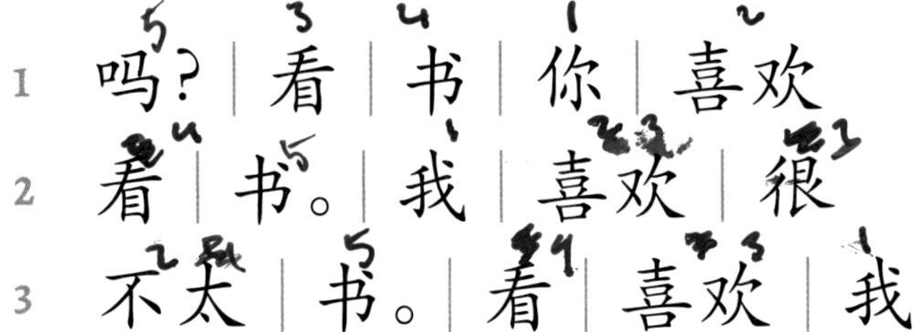

1 吗？| 看 | 书 | 你 | 喜欢
2 看 | 书。| 我 | 喜欢 | 很
3 不太 | 书。| 看 | 喜欢 | 我

Language Reference

3 Action word + action word

In Chinese, verbs can be placed together directly. There is no need to add an ending, like "-ing," to the verb. Also, there is no need to add another word, like "to," between the verbs.

		Verb 1	Verb 2		Meaning
1	我	xǐhuan 喜欢	kàn 看	shū 书。	I like to read.
2	你们	xǐhuan 喜欢	kàn 看	diànshì 电视 吗？	Do you like watching TV?

4 Saying how much you like a thing or activity

Use the words 很 (hěn), 不太 (bú tài), and 不 to talk about how much you like or don't like something.

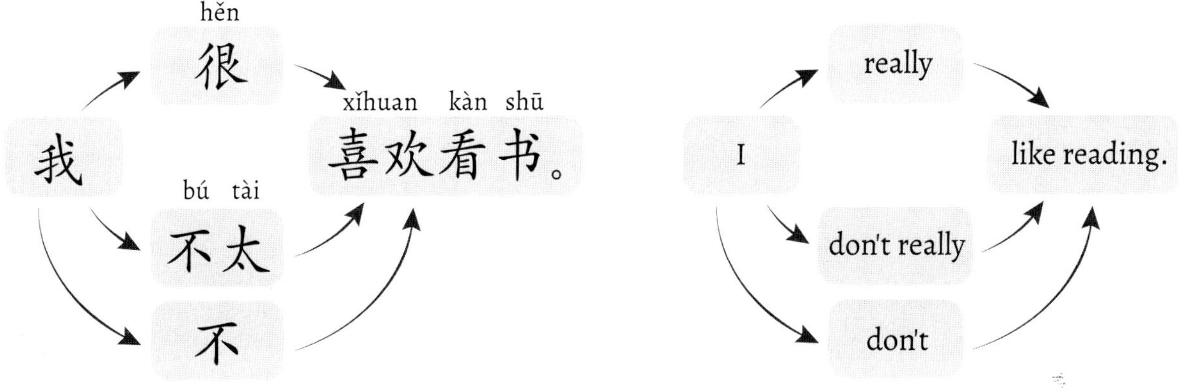

2d Using the Language INTERPERSONAL

Everyone in your class has been assigned one of four secret identities! Carefully read the profiles for the secret identities. Your teacher will let you know which one now belongs to you. Ask your classmates questions like the ones listed below to figure out their secret identities.

- 你有姐姐吗?
- 你喜欢看书吗?

Brothers: 一个哥哥
Sisters: 两个妹妹
Watching TV: 不太喜欢
Reading: 很喜欢

Brothers: 没有
Sisters: 两个妹妹
Watching TV: 很喜欢
Reading: 很喜欢

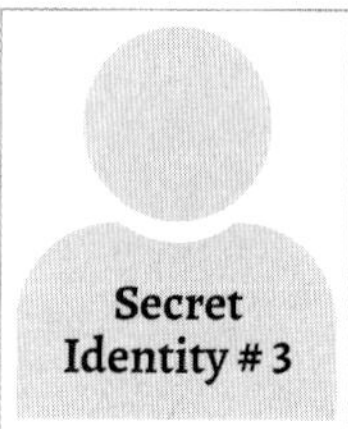

Brothers: 没有
Sisters: 三个妹妹
Watching TV: 不太喜欢
Reading: 很喜欢

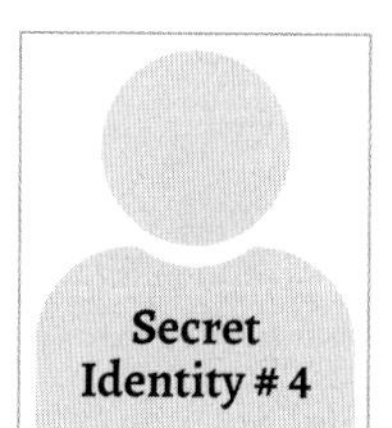

Brothers: 两个哥哥
Sisters: 两个妹妹
Watching TV: 很喜欢
Reading: 很喜欢

When a new technology is invented, a word to describe it must also be invented! In Chinese, new words can be created by combining characters that describe the new technology. In the word 电视, the character 电 means "electricity" or "electric" and the character 视 means "vision." Put them together, and you have "electric vision" or television!

Can you guess what these words mean?

电脑 diàn nǎo = electric brain = ?

电话 diàn huà = electric speech = ?

电影 diàn yǐng = electric shadow = ?

Talking about pets

3a Language Model TARGET LANGUAGE INPUT

Your teacher will lead a discussion about the image below. Try to participate as much as you can. If there is anything you don't understand, let your teacher know.

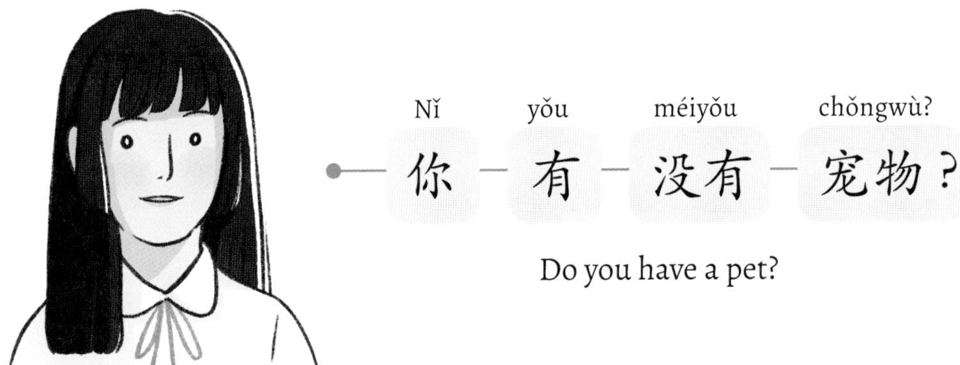

Nǐ yǒu méiyǒu chǒngwù?
你 有 没有 宠物？
Do you have a pet?

A pet store in the city of Hong Kong

3b New Words in Conversation INTERPRETIVE

Audio

Listen to the audio and try to understand as much as you can. Then read the dialogue, using the pinyin text and vocabulary list to figure out unfamiliar words.

小明是你的朋友吗？ — Xiǎomíng shì nǐ de péngyou ma?

他是我的好朋友。 — Tā shì wǒ de hǎo péngyou.

他有没有宠物？ — Tā yǒu méiyǒu chǒngwù?

他没有宠物，可是我有宠物。 — Tā méiyǒu chǒngwù, kěshì wǒ yǒu chǒngwù.

你有几只宠物？ — Nǐ yǒu jǐ zhī chǒngwù?

我有两只宠物。 — Wǒ yǒu liǎng zhī chǒngwù.

我有一只宠物！它是一只猫。 — Wǒ yǒu yì zhī chǒngwù! Tā shì yì zhī māo.

Comprehension Check

		T	F
1	Xiaoming is Owen's friend.	○	○
2	Xiaoming has two pets.	○	○
3	Owen has two pets.	○	○
4	Miko has one pet.	○	○

Vocabulary

	Word	Pinyin	Meaning
16	宠物	chǒngwù	pet (animal)
17	只	zhī	(measure word for some animals)
18	它	tā	it (used for animals and things)
19	猫	māo	cat
20	狗	gǒu	dog
	小明	Xiǎomíng	(a name)

3c Puzzle It Out PROGRESS CHECK

Complete the exercise below to check your understanding of what you learned in Section 3. If you have questions, consult the Language Reference section.

Make correct sentences by rearranging the words in each row.

1 有 | 她 | 宠物。 | 三只

2 几只 | 宠物? | 有 | 你

3 我 | 一只 | 有 | 宠物。

LANGUAGE CHALLENGE

Some common pets, like dogs and snakes, are part of the Chinese zodiac. Find out what animal represents the year you were born and report to the class! Can you learn to say all the zodiac animals in Chinese?

wo you Ye Zhi gǒu

Language Reference

5 Measure words for animals

The measure word 个 can be used for people and many other objects. 只 (zhī) is the measure word used for many, but not all, pets.

1 我有两只宠物。(zhī chǒngwù) I have two pets.

2 你有几只宠物？(zhī chǒngwù) How many pets do you have?

3 我有九只！(zhī) I have nine!

Here are some common pets and the measure words used to count them.

zhī 只			tiáo 条		pǐ 匹
gǒu 狗 dog	māo 猫 cat	tùzi 兔子 rabbit	yú 鱼 fish	shé 蛇 snake	mǎ 马 horse

3d Using the Language INTERPERSONAL

Are you a cat person or a dog person? What about your classmates? Ask your classmates how much they like dogs and cats, and whether or not they have cats or dogs as pets. Use the questions below as a guide.

- 你喜欢狗吗？
- 你喜欢猫吗？
- 你有几只狗？
- 你有几只猫？

Ni you Shema Chongu

Put the Pieces Together!

A Reading and Listening INTERPRETIVE

Audio

Passage 1
ISABELLA AND MARTIN ARE CURIOUS TO LEARN MORE ABOUT DAMING'S FAMILY. IT TURNS OUT HE HAS A VERY PUZZLING YOUNGER BROTHER!

6
他有两个哥哥和一个妹妹。
他不喜欢看书，
他很喜欢看电视！
7
大明，你的弟弟
有一个妹妹。
可是你没有妹妹……
8
你是学生。
可是你的弟弟
不是学生……
9
看，
我的"弟弟"小明！

Comprehension Check

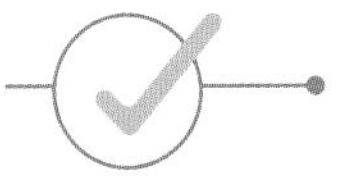

		T	F
1	Daming's younger brother is a student.	○	○
2	Daming's younger brother has a younger sister.	○	○
3	Daming's younger brother likes to read.	○	○
4	Xiaoming is Daming's pet.	○	○

Passage 2 Today is the first day of Chinese class, and these students are getting to know their new teacher. Read the dialogue below. Are the statements that follow true (T) or false (F)?

Teacher: 同学们好！

Students: 老师好！

Student A: 老师，你有宠物吗？

Teacher: 我有一只猫。你喜欢宠物吗？

Student A: 喜欢！

Student B: 老师，你有哥哥吗？

Teacher: 我没有哥哥，可是我有一个弟弟。

Student C: 老师，你是妹妹吗？

Teacher: 我不是妹妹！我是姐姐。

		T	F
1	The teacher has one cat.	○	○
2	Student A doesn't like pets.	○	○
3	The teacher has a younger brother.	○	○
4	The teacher is a younger sister.	○	○

Passage 3 Your mom just bought these outfits for her friend, who has two new babies. Are the babies girls or boys?

Passage 4 Listen to the personal introduction and answer the following questions.

1 Does the speaker have older siblings?
 (a) Yes, the speaker has an older brother and an older sister.
 (b) Yes, the speaker has an older brother and two older sisters.
 (c) Yes, the speaker has an older brother but no older sister.

2 Does the speaker have younger siblings?
 (a) No, the speaker does not have younger siblings.
 (b) Yes, the speaker has a younger brother.
 (c) Yes, the speaker has a younger sister.

3 Who likes watching TV?
 (a) The speaker likes watching TV.
 (b) The speaker's older brother likes watching TV.
 (c) The speaker's pet likes watching TV.

Passage 5 Listen as the speaker describes her friend's family. Are the following questions true (T) or false (F)?

		T	F
1	The speaker is friends with the boy in the picture.	○	○
2	The girl in the picture is named Chunchun.	○	○
3	Everyone in the family really likes their pet.	○	○

On a separate piece of paper, write four sentences describing your own likes and dislikes. Then share your sentences with your group and ask your group members about what they like and dislike. Who are you most similar to in your group?

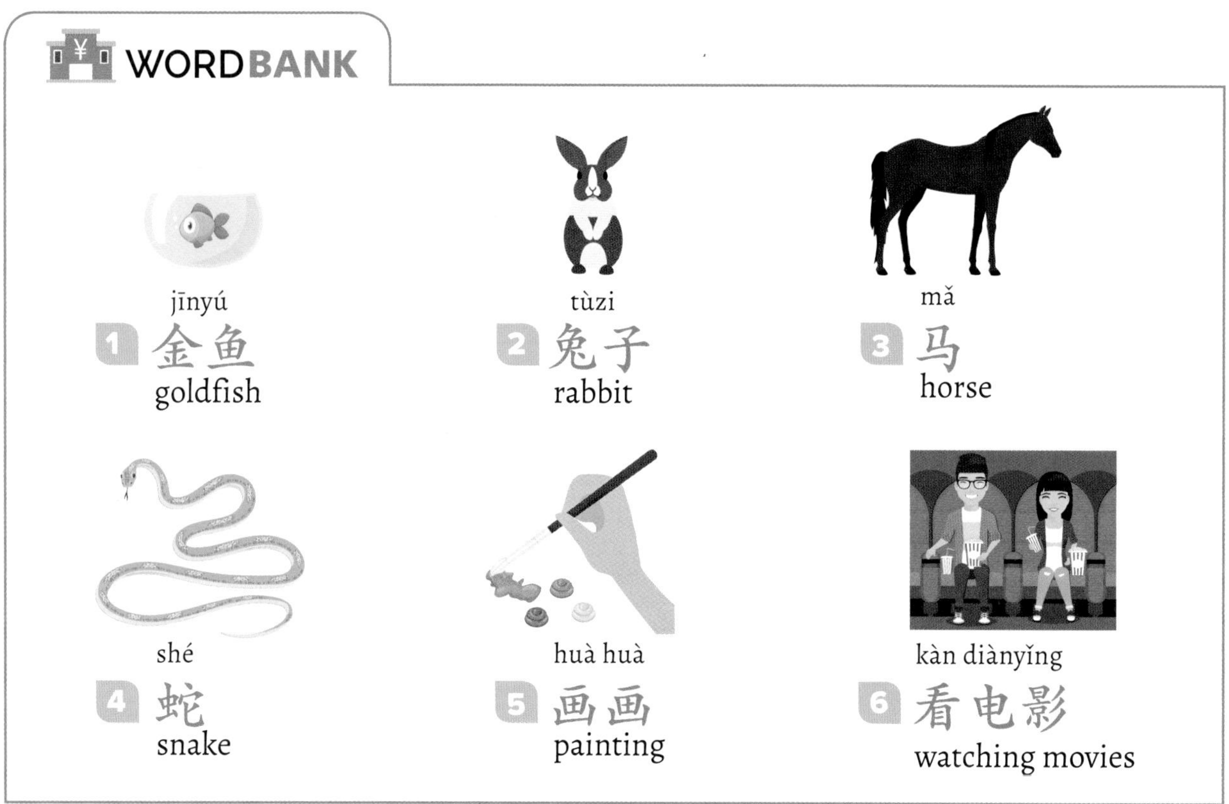

C Final Project PRESENTATIONAL

The Animal Party

You and your classmates are planning a pet-themed party. All your classmates and their siblings are invited. To plan the party, you need to find out what pets everyone likes.

Step 1: Discuss which pets you like and dislike with the classmates in your group. Then pick at least three pets that you all like.

Step 2: Interview your classmates to find out if they and their siblings like the pets that your group chose in Step 1. Keep a tally of how many people like each type of pet.

Step 3: Create charts like the sample below to show how many people like and dislike each type of pet. Pick the most popular animal for the theme of your party.

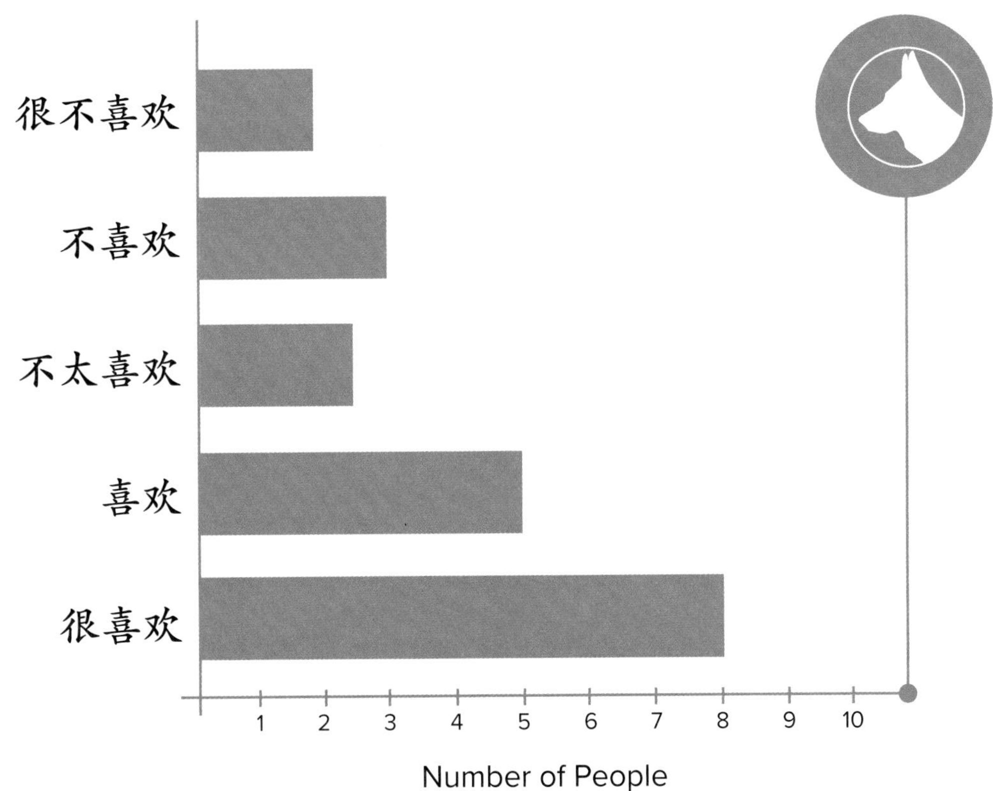

Can-Do Goals

Talk with your teacher if you have questions or if you are not certain you can do the following tasks:

- Understand simple descriptions of families
- Ask and answer questions about family members
- Express how many siblings and pets you have
- Understand when others talk about their likes and dislikes
- Talk about likes and dislikes
- Use different measure words to talk about people and animals

Cultural Knowledge

What are some ways that family life in China is changing?

A family in the city of Shanghai looks at a photo on a cell phone during the Chinese New Year holiday.

EXPLORING A NEW PLACE

In Unit 2, you will learn to talk about studying, sports, and music. You will also learn to ask and answer questions about where things happen.

UNIT 2

第 dì
二 èr
单 dān
元 yuán

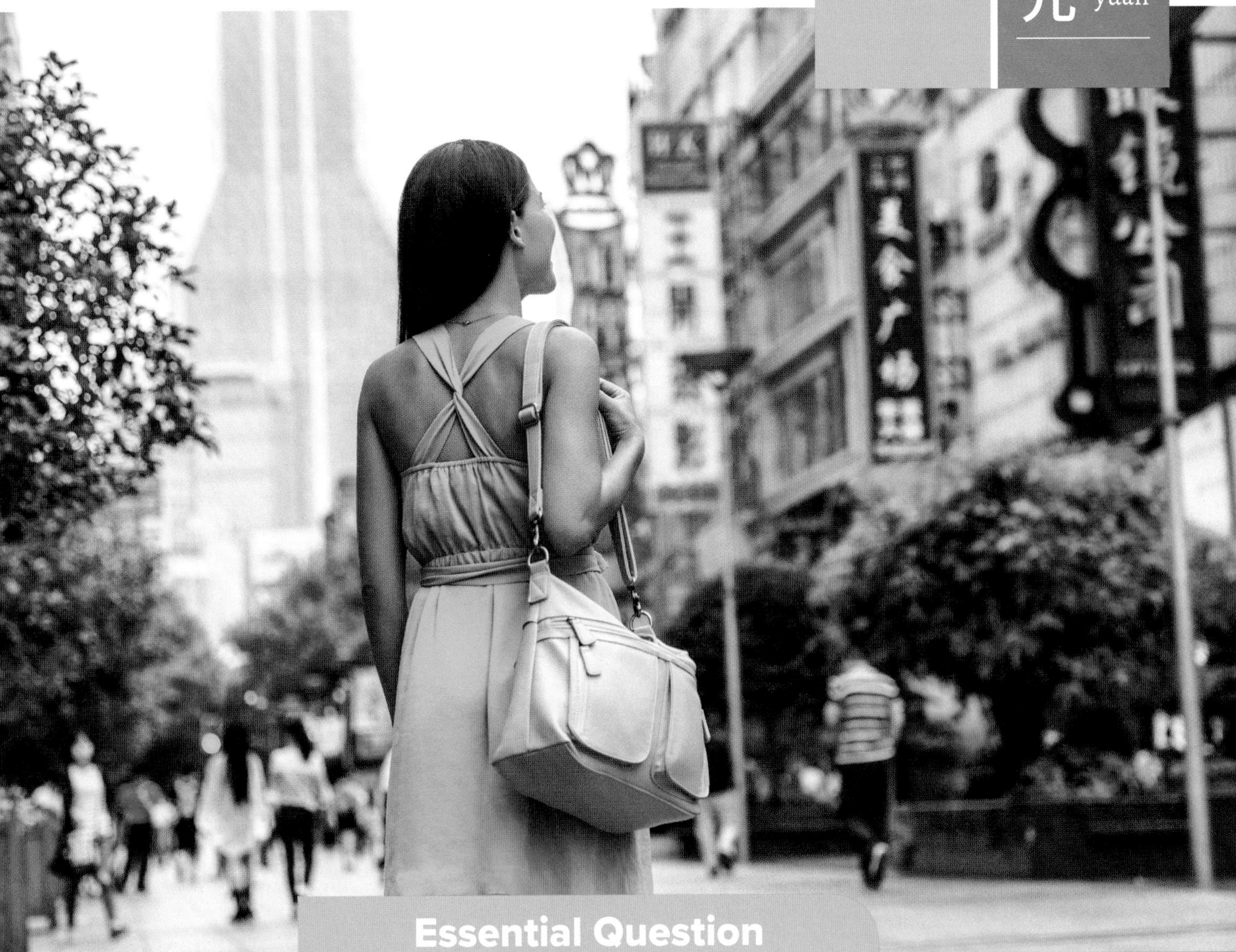

Essential Question

How does where you live affect what you do?

CHAPTER 4
Goodbye America, Hello China!

The Lopezes are finally on their way to China! But not everyone is excited about it.

CHAPTER 5
Sports in the Neighborhood

Isabella and Martin explore their new Beijing neighborhood and its many sports facilities.

CHAPTER 6
Appreciating New Sounds

Martin, Daming, and Isabella all decide to take up a new instrument.

UNIT 2 PROJECT

At the end of the unit, you will imagine that you are going to attend a summer program in Beijing, and you need to select the school you're going to attend. You will:

- Examine flyers for the schools and get to know the neighborhoods they are in and classes they offer
- Work in groups to trade information about the schools and discuss which you like best
- Tell the class about the school you have chosen, what classes you can take, and what you can do in the neighborhood

Goodbye America, Hello China!

CHAPTER 4 第 dì 四 sì 课 kè

Martin: I just finished packing. I can't believe that we'll be in China in a couple of days!

Isabella: Yeah, that feels weird.

Martin: Daming will be on our flight. I hope he'll be able to answer our questions about Beijing!

Isabella: Yeah...

Martin: Aren't you excited to explore Beijing?

Isabella: I guess so...I'll miss my friends in the U.S., though.

Can-Do Goals

In this chapter, you will learn to:

- Describe something that two or more people have in common
- Understand where someone is and say where you are
- Ask someone to make a choice between two options
- Use "this" and "that" to refer to things if you do not know the words in Chinese
- Talk about your location now and your location this week

CULTURE CONNECTION

Běijīng, wǒ de lǎojiā

北京，我的老家

Beijing, My Hometown

On the flight, Daming tells Isabella and Martin a little about his 老家 (lǎojiā), or hometown, of Beijing. The city has been inhabited for thousands of years and has been China's capital for most of the past 800 years. This photo shows Beijing's Forbidden City, which was the home of Chinese emperors from 1420 until the early 20th century.

Let's Go to the Opera

Beijing is an important cultural center and is home to one of China's most famous art forms — Beijing opera, known as 京剧 (jīngjù). Beijing opera performers, such as the ones pictured here, tell stories through song and dance.

Ancient...but Modern, Too

Beijing may be an ancient city, but it also has modern activities. The city's residents can enjoy amusement parks and explore a great shopping scene. This mall, known simply as "The Place," has many attractions, including shops, international restaurants, and a massive outdoor screen with an ever-changing display.

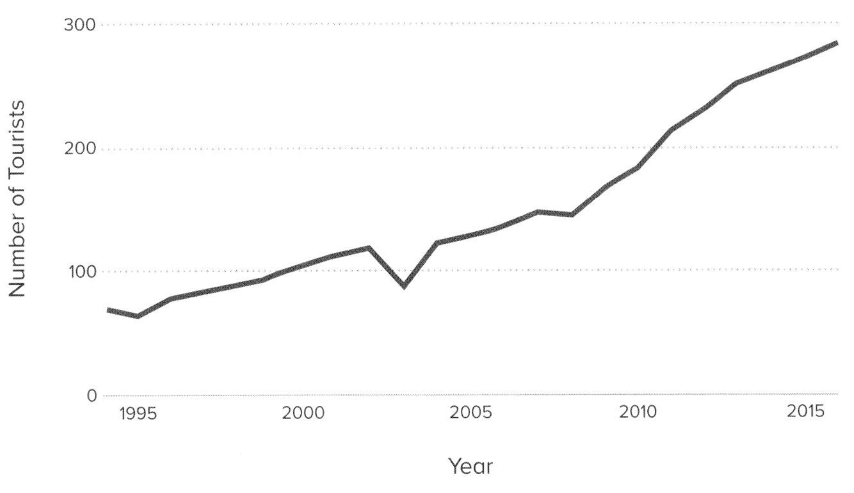

By the Numbers

Whether drawn by the city's long history or looking to explore more modern attractions, millions of international and Chinese tourists visit Beijing every year.

Source: Beijing Statistical Yearbook 2017

REFLECT ON THE ESSENTIAL QUESTION

How does where you live affect what you do?

1. What is the capital city of your country famous for? How do you think it is similar to or different from Beijing?
2. What would you suggest people do or see when visiting your hometown?
3. How would your life change if you moved to a different city? A different country?

Talking about groups

1a Language Model TARGET LANGUAGE INPUT

Your teacher will lead a discussion about the image below. Try to participate as much as you can. If there is anything you don't understand, let your teacher know.

Tāmen dōu xǐhuan kàn shū!
他们 — 都 — 喜欢 — 看 — 书!

They both/all like reading!

Nǐ xǐhuan kàn shū ma?
你 — 喜欢 — 看 — 书 — 吗?

Do you like reading?

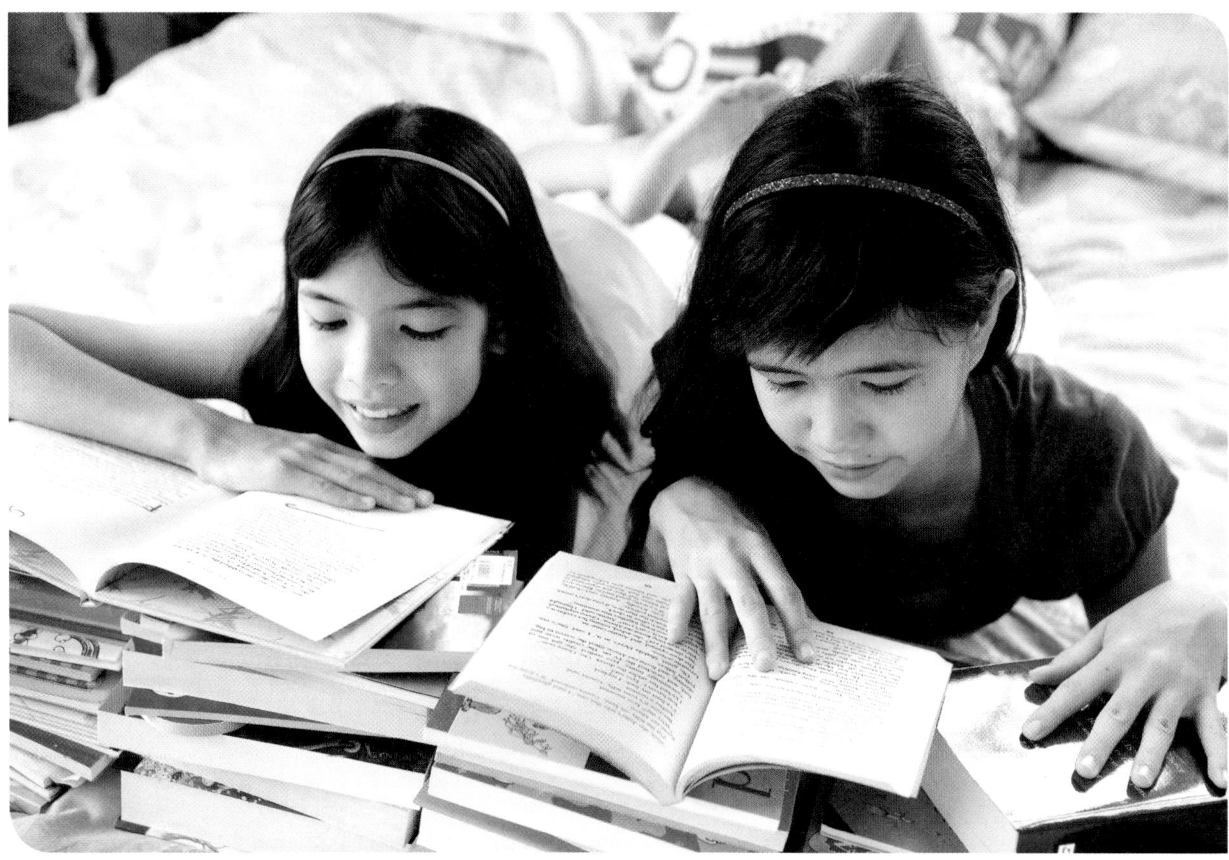

1b New Words in Conversation INTERPRETIVE

Listen to the audio and try to understand as much as you can. Then read the dialogue, using the pinyin text and vocabulary list to figure out unfamiliar words.

我们都喜欢学中文，对不对？ — Wǒmen dōu xǐhuan xué Zhōngwén, duì bú duì?

对，我很喜欢学中文！ — Duì, wǒ hěn xǐhuan xué Zhōngwén!

不对，我不太喜欢学中文……可是我很喜欢中国。 — Bú duì, wǒ bú tài xǐhuan xué Zhōngwén . . . Kěshì wǒ hěn xǐhuan Zhōngguó.

我也很喜欢中国。 — Wǒ yě hěn xǐhuan Zhōngguó.

我们都是美国人。我们也都很喜欢中国！ — Wǒmen dōu shì Měiguó rén. Wǒmen yě dōu hěn xǐhuan Zhōngguó!

Comprehension Check

		T	F
1	Maya and Owen both like studying Chinese.		
2	Sanjay also likes studying Chinese.		
3	Maya, Owen, and Sanjay all like China.		
4	Maya, Owen, and Sanjay are all Americans.		

Audio

Vocabulary

	Word	Pinyin	Meaning
1	都	dōu	all, both
2	学	xué	to learn, to study
3	对	duì	right, correct
4	中国	Zhōngguó	China
5	美国	Měiguó	United States of America
6	人	rén	person, people

1c Puzzle It Out PROGRESS CHECK

Complete the exercise below to check your understanding of what you learned in Section 1. If you have questions, consult the Language Reference section.

Make correct sentences by rearranging the words and phrases in each row.

1 都 | 学英文。 | 我们 | 喜欢

2 她和他 | 中国人。 | 是 | 都

3 不喜欢 | 你们 | 都 | 吗？ | 看电视

4 是 | 他们 | 都 | 吗？ | 学生

Language Reference

1 Using 都 to say "all" or "both"

The word 都 (dōu) can mean either "both" or "all." Note that 都 (dōu) always comes after the subject and before the verb.

dōu Měiguó rén

1 我们都是美国人。

We are both/all Americans.

dōu

2 你和你的弟弟都喜欢看书吗?

Do you and your younger brother both like to read books?

The meaning of 都没有 and 都不 is similar to "neither" or "none." By contrast, 不都 means "not all."

dōu

3 她和她的朋友都没有宠物。

Neither she nor her friend has a pet.

dōu

4 我们不都有宠物。

We do not all have pets. (Only some of us have pets.)

dōu

5 他们都不喜欢看电视。

Neither/none of them likes to watch TV.

dōu

6 他们不都喜欢看电视。

Not all of them like to watch TV. (Only some of them like to watch TV.)

1d Using the Language INTERPERSONAL

In small groups, take turns making statements that are true for everyone in the group. If a classmate makes a statement that is not true for you, you should contradict that statement. Then the person who made the incorrect statement is out of the game.

A: 我们都喜欢看电视。

B: 不对！ 我不喜欢看电视。

[A is now out.]

The Chinese names for many countries sound similar to their English names. One example is the Chinese name for Italy, 意大利 (Yìdàlì). For other countries, such as 美国 (Měiguó), the name is a single character paired with 国 (guó), which means "country." Try to match the countries listed below to the letters marked on the map.

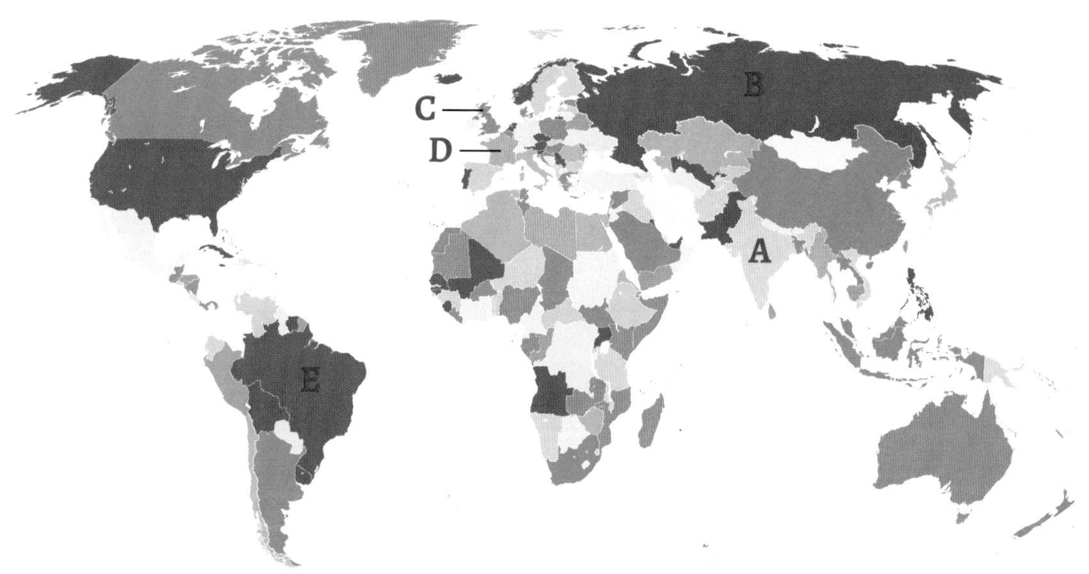

1 英国 (Yīngguó)

2 俄罗斯 (Éluósī)

3 法国 (Fǎguó)

4 巴西 (Bāxī)

5 印度 (Yìndù)

Using 还是 to ask questions

2a Language Model TARGET LANGUAGE INPUT

Your teacher will lead a discussion about the images below. Try to participate as much as you can. If there is anything you don't understand, let your teacher know.

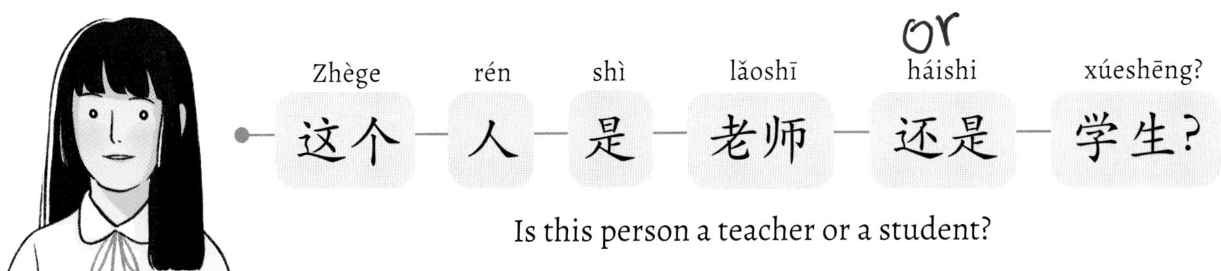

Zhège rén shì lǎoshī háishi xúeshēng?
这个 人 是 老师 还是 学生?

Is this person a teacher or a student?

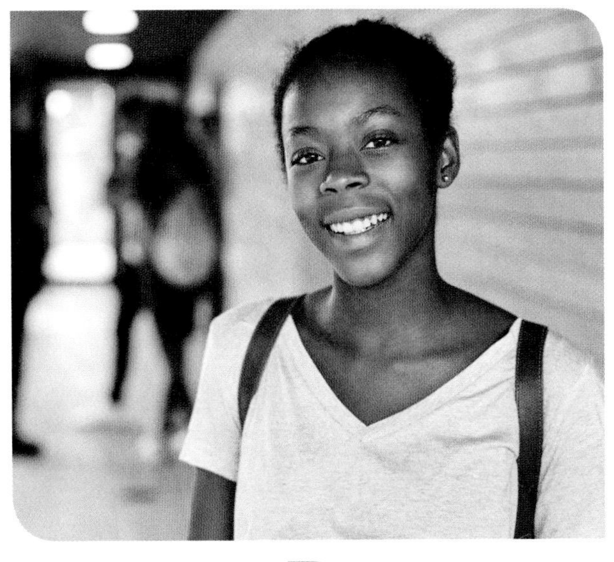

1

zhège rén
这个人
this person

2

nàge rén
那个人
that person

Audio

2b New Words in Conversation

INTERPRETIVE

Listen to the audio and try to understand as much as you can of Miko and Ellen's conversation as they look at a photograph. Then read the dialogue, using the pinyin text and vocabulary list to figure out unfamiliar words.

这个人是谁？你知道吗？ — Zhège rén shì shéi? Nǐ zhīdào ma?

他是白大明。 — Tā shì Bái Dàmíng.

他是北京人吗？ — Tā shì Běijīng rén ma?

他是北京人。 — Tā shì Běijīng rén.

那个人是他姐姐还是他妹妹？ — Nàge rén shì tā jiějie háishi tā mèimei?

他没有姐姐，也没有妹妹。那个人是大明的朋友。 — Tā méiyǒu jiějie, yě méiyǒu mèimei. Nàge rén shì Dàmíng de péngyǒu.

Comprehension Check

		T	F
1	Ellen does not know who Daming is.	○	○
2	Ellen tells Miko that Daming is from Beijing.	○	○
3	Daming has an older sister.	○	○

Vocabulary

Audio

	Word	Pinyin	Meaning
7	这	zhè	this
8	知道	zhīdào	to know
9	北京	Běijīng	Beijing
10	那	nà	that
11	还是	háishi	or (in questions)

2c Puzzle It Out PROGRESS CHECK

Complete the exercise below to check your understanding of what you learned in Section 2. If you have questions, consult the Language Reference section.

Use the words in the list to complete the translation of the dialogue. You may use some words more than once.

这
还是
那

A: 这 个人是她哥哥 还是 她弟弟?
Is this person her older brother or her younger brother?

B: 这 个人是她哥哥。那 个人是她弟弟。
This person is her older brother. That person is her younger brother.

2 Pointing things out with 这 and 那

这 (zhè) and 那 (nà) are very similar to the English words "this" and "that." Usually, 这 (zhè) refers to something close to the speaker, while 那 (nà) refers to something that is farther away. When these words are followed by a noun, there is always a measure word in between.

	这/那	Measure Word	Noun	Meaning
1	zhè 这	个	人	this person
2	zhè 这	只	狗	this dog
3	nà 那	个	学生的名字	that student's name

TAKE NOTE

这个 (zhège) and 那个 (nàge) can be used without being followed by any nouns. In these situations, 这个 (zhège) means "this one," and 那个 (nàge) means "that one."

A: 你喜欢这个(zhège)吗？ (pointing at an item)

Do you like this one?

B: 我不喜欢这个(zhège)。

我喜欢那个(nàge)。 (pointing at another item)

I don't like this one. I like that one.

3 Using 还是 to prompt a choice

When asking someone to make a choice, 还是 (háishi) is used between the two options. In this kind of question, the meaning of 还是 (háishi) is similar to the English word "or."

		Option A	还是	Option B	Meaning
1	你喜欢	看书	háishi 还是	看电视?	Do you like to read books or watch TV?
2	她是	你姐姐	háishi 还是	你妹妹?	Is she your older sister or your younger sister?

你姐姐 has the same meaning as 你的姐姐. The 的 is often left out when it comes between a pronoun, like 你, 她, or 我, and someone/something closely related to that person.

我的朋友→我朋友 my friend

她的同学→她同学 her classmate

What a Character!

kǒu
口

1 口 2 口 3 口

口 (kǒu) means "mouth" or "an opening." It is both a character and a component of other characters.

Can you find 口 (kǒu) in each character below?

1 吗 2 知 3 叫 4 同 5 可 6 名 7 哪

2d Using the Language INTERPERSONAL

Imagine that your class is planning a trip to Beijing on a budget. You only have enough money to select one of each option below. Point to each image below and ask which food or form of entertainment the students in your group like best. Tally the results and list the three options that received the most votes.

你喜欢这个还是那个?

A1

Tanghulu is a sweet treat made of candied fruits served on a skewer.

vs.

A2

These beautiful figurines are candy made by crafting melted sugar into delicate shapes.

B1

For hot pot, bite-sized raw foods are cooked in a boiling pot of broth and then taken out and eaten with a dipping sauce.

vs.

B2

Peking duck is a traditional Beijing dish of roasted duck meat with a tasty sweetened skin.

C1

The Beijing Opera Troupe tells classic Chinese stories through song.

vs.

C2

The Beijing Acrobatics Troupe amazes audiences with traditional Chinese acrobatic feats.

Asking about locations

3a Language Model TARGET LANGUAGE INPUT

Your teacher will lead a discussion about the images below. Try to participate as much as you can. If there is anything you don't understand, let your teacher know.

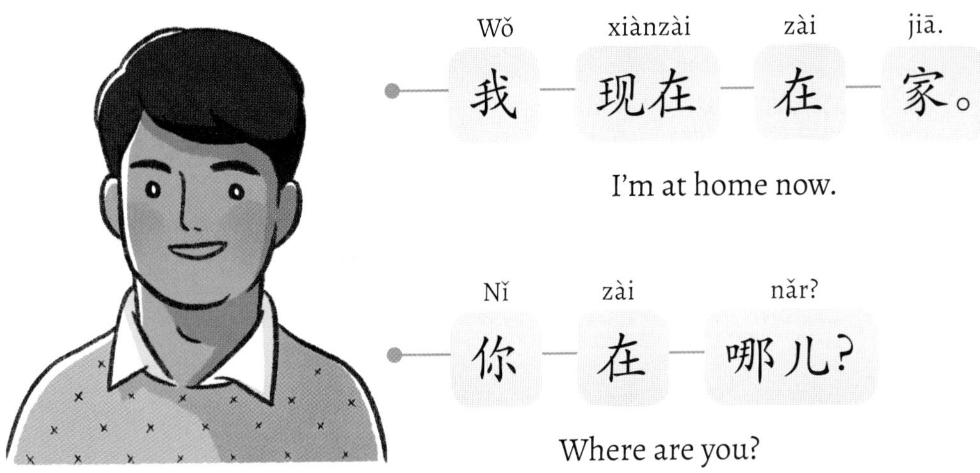

Wǒ xiànzài zài jiā.

我现在在家。

I'm at home now.

Nǐ zài nǎr?

你在哪儿?

Where are you?

1

jiā

家

home

2

xuéxiào

学校

school

Audio

3b New Words in Conversation INTERPRETIVE

Listen to the audio and try to understand as much as you can. Then read the dialogue, using the pinyin text and vocabulary list to figure out unfamiliar words.

Leo, 你在哪儿？
你在我们小区吗？

Leo, nǐ zài nǎr?
Nǐ zài wǒmen xiǎoqū ma?

不在，我在一个美国学校。

Bú zài, wǒ zài yí gè Měiguó xuéxiào.

你现在不在北京吗？

Nǐ xiànzài bú zài Běijīng ma?

对，我这个星期不在家，
不在北京。

Duì, wǒ zhège xīngqī bú zài jiā,
bú zài Běijīng.

Comprehension Check

		T	F
1	Leo is at home.	○	●
2	Leo is at an American school.	●	○
3	Leo will spend this whole week in Beijing.	○	●

Audio

Vocabulary

	Word	Pinyin	Meaning
12	在	zài	to be at, to be in (a place)
13	哪儿	nǎr	where
14	小区	xiǎoqū	neighborhood, apartment complex
15	学校	xuéxiào	school
16	现在	xiànzài	now, at this time
17	星期	xīngqī	week
18	家	jiā	home

3c Puzzle It Out PROGRESS CHECK

Complete the exercises below to check your understanding of what you learned in Section 3. If you have questions, consult the Language Reference section.

Exercise 1 Make correct sentences by rearranging the words in each row.

1 在 | 你 | 吗? | 家

2 朋友 | 在 | 他 | 北京。

3 不 | 我们 | 中国。 | 在

4 哥哥 | 在 | 哪儿? | 你

5 她 | 这个 | 美国。 | 星期 | 在

Exercise 2 Where in the following sentences can 现在 be added?

1 我 (1) 在美国 (2)。

(a) 现在 can only be added where (1) is.

(b) 现在 can only be added where (2) is.

2 她 (1) 妹妹 (2) 在北京。

(a) 现在 can be added where (1) is.

(b) 现在 can be added where (2) is.

3 (1) 他们 (2) 在家。

(a) 现在 can only be added where (1) is.

(b) 现在 can be added either where (1) is or where (2) is.

4 Using 在 to say where you are

When talking about one's location in English, we use the verb "to be" together with either "in" or "at." For example, "I am in Beijing" or "He is at home." In Chinese only one word, 在 (zài), is needed.

	在	Place	Meaning
1 我	zài 在	北京。	I am in Beijing.
2 他	zài 在	xuéxiào 学校。	He is at school.
3 他们	zài 在	jiā 家。	They are at home.

5 Word order with time expressions

In English, time words often go at the end of a sentence, as in the sentence "I am at school now." However, in Chinese the time word can come either before or after the subject but cannot be placed at the end of the sentence.

1 我现在在美国。(xiànzài zài) I am in America now.

2 她这个星期在北京。(xīngqī zài) She is in Beijing this week.

3 现在他在中国。(Xiànzài zài) He is in China now.

3d Using the Language INTERPERSONAL

Imagine that your school has prepared a special summer program. You will be spending one week in Beijing, one week at home, and two weeks at school in your home country. Your teacher will assign each of your classmates to one of the four different program groups. Pair up and find out which group your partner is in by pointing to different weeks on the calendar.

Example:

Student A: 你这个星期在哪儿?

Student B: 我这个星期在家。

AUGUST

	SUNDAY	MONDAY	TUESDAY	WEDNESDAY	THURSDAY	FRIDAY	SATURDAY
							1
Week 1	2	3	4	5	6	7	8
Week 2	9	10	11	12	13	14	15
Week 3	16	17	18	19	20	21	22
Week 4	23	24	25	26	27	28	29
	30	31					

Group A

Week 1: 在北京

Week 2: 在家

Week 3: 在学校

Week 4: 在学校

Group B

Week 1: 在北京

Week 2: 在学校

Week 3: 在学校

Week 4: 在家

Group C

Week 1: 在家

Week 2: 在学校

Week 3: 在学校

Week 4: 在北京

Group D

Week 1: 在家

Week 2: 在北京

Week 3: 在学校

Week 4: 在学校

Have you ever volunteered to help your neighbors, or wanted to do so? Imagine that your new neighbor only speaks Chinese. Draw a simple map of your town or neighborhood. Mark your home and school on the map and research how to say other useful locations in Chinese. Practice using 这 and 那 to point out places on your map to your classmates.

A girl holding a sign that reads "Welcome" in Chinese

CHAPTER 4

Put the Pieces Together!

A Reading and Listening INTERPRETIVE

Audio

Passage 1

EMMA, ISABELLA, AND MARTIN ARE ON THE PLANE. DAMING WALKS ON AND TAKES HIS SEAT NEXT TO ISABELLA.

5
这是我的朋友 Matt。

6
你看，Matt、Aria
和我在我们学校。

7
我的朋友都在美国，
他们都是美国人。
我喜欢中国，可是我
没有中国朋友……

8
不对，你有中国朋友。
我的中国朋友是谁？

9
我知道，我们的
中国朋友是大明，
对不对？
对，我们有
一个中国朋友！

10
SHOP
MUSIC

11

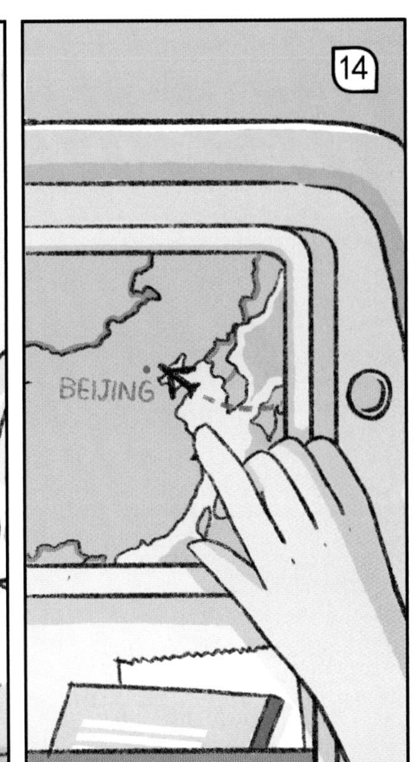

Comprehension Check 

	T	F
1 Isabella likes learning Chinese.	○	○
2 Isabella shows Daming a picture of her English teacher.	○	○
3 Isabella has no Chinese friends.	○	○
4 At the end of the dialogue, they are all still in America.	○	○

Passage 2 Imagine that you just arrived in Beijing for a short-term language program. From the school bus, you see this traffic sign ahead. What word do you recognize on this sign? What do you think this sign might mean?

Audio

Passage 3 Ellen is calling Owen's house to see if he would like to visit the Forbidden City. Listen to the dialogue and answer the following questions.

1 Who is Ellen talking to?

(a) Owen

(b) Owen's brother

(c) Owen's dad

2 Where is Owen this week?

(a) He's in China.

(b) He's at home.

(c) He's in the U.S.

B Speaking INTERPERSONAL

Daming's hometown, or 老家 (lǎojiā), is 北京. Learn about where your classmates' parents are from. Use these questions:

你爸爸的老家在哪儿?
你妈妈的老家在哪儿?

Keep track of which country, state, and city each of your classmates' parents are from. How many of your classmates' parents are from the same state(s) as your parents?

C Final Project PRESENTATIONAL

Journalism Internship

Your class has been recruited as journalism interns for a news website. Imagine that your assignment is to interview one important person. You need to pick some people who are newsworthy and figure out where they are, so that you know where you will go to interview them. In groups, suggest some people (such as politicians, sports figures, and singers) and ask in Chinese whether the students in your group know and like them.

Step 1: Pick two people that everyone in the group knows and likes.

Step 2: Find pictures of these two people and research where you think they are this week.

Step 3: Create a poster with the pictures. Under each picture, write the person's name and a sentence in Chinese describing the person's location this week.

Step 4: Present your poster and use 还是 to ask your classmates which important person they like.

Step 5: Imagine that you will go "on assignment" to the location of the person who got the most "likes" from your classmates. Each group will tell the class where they will be by completing this sentence:

我们这个星期在 ____________。

Can-Do Goals

Talk with your teacher if you have questions or if you are not certain you can do the following tasks:

- Describe something that two or more people have in common
- Understand where someone is and say where you are
- Ask someone to make a choice between two options
- Use "this" and "that" to refer to things if you do not know the words in Chinese
- Talk about your location now and your location this week

Cultural Knowledge

What is your impression of Beijing?

A view of the Summer Palace, a site featuring imperial gardens and traditional Chinese architecture.

Sports in the Neighborhood

CHAPTER 5

第 dì 五 wǔ 课 kè

The Lopezes have moved into their apartment in Beijing. Now that she has finally adjusted to the new time zone, Isabella is looking for things to do.

Isabella: Mom, I'm bored. I don't want to be stuck at home all the time.

Emma: There are a lot of activities in the neighborhood.

Isabella: Really? Is there a softball field?

Emma: No, but there are other options.

Martin: Maybe Daming can give us a tour of the neighborhood later today?

Emma: Yes, that's a good idea!

Can-Do Goals

In this chapter you will learn to:

- Name some sports that are popular in China
- Discuss which sports you can play
- Say where you play sports
- Express whether or not you want to play a sport
- Understand the sports others can and want to play
- Ask if others want to play or watch sports

CULTURE CONNECTION

体育运动 (tǐyù yùndòng)

Sports & Exercise

Staying healthy is important, and the Chinese government has made a commitment to encouraging an active lifestyle for people of all ages.

More than a Walk in the Park

The Chinese government has used funds from the sale of lottery tickets to place exercise equipment, called 健身路径 (jiànshēn lùjìng), in parks and neighborhoods across China. These free "outdoor gyms" are especially popular among older citizens, as can be seen in this Beijing park.

Here, middle school students in Hebei Province participate in group exercises. This kind of daily, synchronized physical activity is common in Chinese schools.

Fit for School

Every year, millions of Chinese middle schoolers take a multi-day test to get into high school. One portion of the test assesses physical fitness. Students are asked to do a range of tasks, such as dribbling a basketball around a course, doing sit-ups or pull-ups, or throwing a 2 kg (4.4 lb) medicine ball.

By the Numbers

A survey conducted by the Chinese government in 2014 showed that 94.6% of Chinese people aged 6 to 19 exercised or played sports at least once a week either at school or outside of school. Some of the most popular sports were distance running, basketball, badminton, and ping-pong.

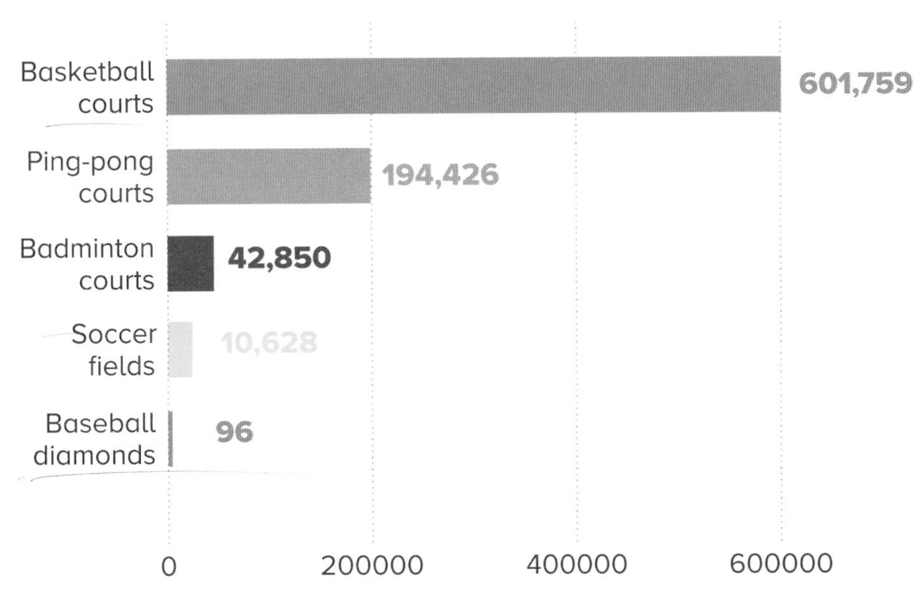

Source: General Administration of Sport of China, 2013

REFLECT ON THE ESSENTIAL QUESTION

How does where you live affect what you do?

1. Which sports are popular in China? Are these sports also popular where you live?
2. What role do sports and exercise play in schools in your area? How do you think it compares to Chinese schools?
3. What kinds of athletic fields and facilities are available in your community? How does that affect what kinds of activities you can do?

Playing sports

1a Language Model TARGET LANGUAGE INPUT

Your teacher will lead a discussion about the images below. Try to participate as much as you can. If there is anything you don't understand, let your teacher know.

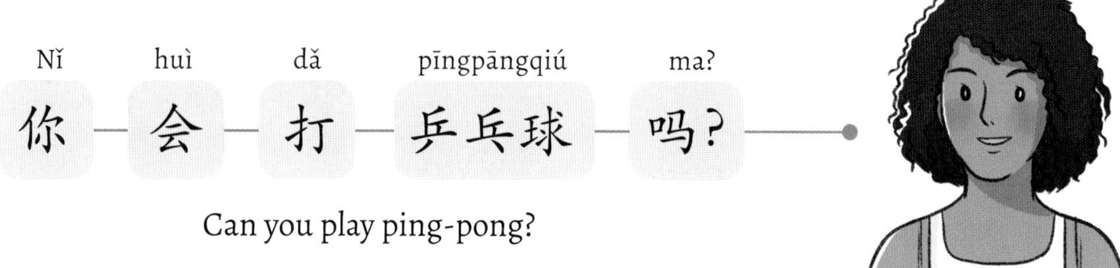

Nǐ huì dǎ pīngpāngqiú ma?
你 会 打 乒乓球 吗?

Can you play ping-pong?

1

dǎ pīngpāngqiú
打乒乓球
play ping-pong

2

dǎ lánqiú
打篮球
play basketball

3

dǎ wǎngqiú
打网球
play tennis

4

tī zúqiú
踢足球
play soccer

1b New Words in Conversation INTERPRETIVE

Listen to the audio and try to understand as much as you can. Then read the dialogue, using the pinyin text and vocabulary list to figure out unfamiliar words.

你会打篮球吗？ Nǐ **huì dǎ lánqiú** ma?

我不会打篮球。 Wǒ bú **huì dǎ lánqiú**.

你会打乒乓球吗？ Nǐ **huì dǎ pīngpāngqiú** ma?

我也不太会打乒乓球。 Wǒ yě bú tài **huì dǎ pīngpāngqiú**.
我会踢足球。 Wǒ **huì tī zúqiú**.

我会踢足球，也会打网球。 Wǒ **huì tī zúqiú**, yě **huì dǎ wǎngqiú**.

Comprehension Check

		T	F
1	Sanjay can't play basketball.	○	○
2	Maya can only play soccer.	○	○

Vocabulary

	Word	Pinyin	Meaning
1	会	huì	can, know how to
2	打	dǎ	to hit, to play (basketball, ping-pong)
3	篮球	lánqiú	basketball (the game and the object)
4	乒乓球	pīngpāngqiú	ping-pong, table tennis; ping-pong ball
5	踢	tī	to kick, to play (soccer)
6	足球	zúqiú	soccer; soccer ball
7	网球	wǎngqiú	tennis; tennis ball

1c Puzzle It Out PROGRESS CHECK

Complete the exercise below to check your understanding of what you learned in Section 1. If you have questions, consult the Language Reference section.

Make correct sentences by rearranging the words and phrases in each row.

1 足球。| 我 | 踢 | 会

2 会 | 你 | 打 | 不会 | 篮球？

3 他 | 吗？ | 乒乓球 | 打 | 会

4 不太 | 打 | 她 | 网球。 | 会

Language Reference

1 Using 会 to say what you can do

In Chinese, the word 会 (huì) is used to express that you can do something. This word is usually used when you have learned how to do a skill or an activity.

Q: 你会打篮球吗？ (huì dǎ lánqiú)	Can you play basketball?
A1: 不会。 (huì)	No (I can't).
A2: 不太会。 (huì)	Not really. / I'm not good at it.
A3: 我很会打篮球！ (huì dǎ lánqiú)	I'm really good at basketball!

2 Different words for playing sports

In Chinese, the word used for playing a certain sport varies depending on the most important action in the sport. 打 (dǎ), which means "to hit," is used with many sports. However, 踢 (tī), which means "to kick," is used for soccer.

1	huì dǎ pīngpāngqiú 我会打乒乓球。	I can play ping-pong.
2	tī zúqiú 我喜欢踢足球。	I like to play soccer.

1d Using the Language INTERPERSONAL

What sports can your classmates play? Pick one sport and interview your whole class to find out who can play it. How many students can play that sport? When you've finished, share your findings with the class. Which sport is played by the most people in your class?

Example:

A: 你会打篮球吗？

B: 不会。 (A writes down B's response.)

B: 你会踢足球吗？

A: 我不太会踢足球。 (B writes down A's response.)

(Both A and B go on to interview other students.)

Sports aren't the only games enjoyed around the world. Rock, Paper, Scissors, for example, is also played in China. The game is called 石头 (shítou) 剪刀 (jiǎndāo) 布 (bù) in China, which means "rock, scissors, fabric." Chinese students say "shítou jiǎndāo bù!" and throw out their hands just as they say the last word. Try playing it this way with a classmate!

Describing a place using 有

2a Language Model TARGET LANGUAGE INPUT

Your teacher will lead a discussion about the image below. Try to participate as much as you can. If there is anything you don't understand, let your teacher know.

Nàr	yǒu	zúqiú	chǎng.
那儿	有	足球	场。

There is a soccer field (over there).

Nǐ	xiǎng	tī	zúqiú	ma?
你	想	踢	足球	吗？

Do you want to play soccer?

2b New Words in Conversation INTERPRETIVE

Listen to the audio and try to understand as much as you can. Then read the dialogue, using the pinyin text and vocabulary list to figure out unfamiliar words.

这儿有一个篮球场。那儿有一个足球场。你们想去打篮球还是踢足球？

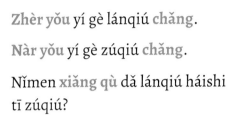

Zhèr yǒu yí gè lánqiú chǎng. Nàr yǒu yí gè zúqiú chǎng. Nǐmen xiǎng qù dǎ lánqiú háishi tī zúqiú?

我想去打篮球。我觉得打篮球很有意思。

Wǒ xiǎng qù dǎ lánqiú. Wǒ juéde dǎ lánqiú hěn yǒuyìsi.

我不会打篮球。我想踢足球。

Wǒ bú huì dǎ lánqiú. Wǒ xiǎng tī zúqiú.

Comprehension Check

	T	F
1 Miko asks if her friends want to play tennis or soccer.	○	○
2 Ellen wants to play soccer.	○	○
3 Ellen thinks basketball is boring.	○	○
4 Sanjay can't play basketball.	○	○
5 Sanjay doesn't want to play soccer.	○	○

Audio

Vocabulary

	Word	Pinyin	Meaning
8	这儿	zhèr	here, over here
9	有	yǒu	there is, there are
10	场	chǎng	outdoor court or field (for sports)
11	那儿	nàr	there, over there
12	想	xiǎng	to want (to do something)
13	去	qù	to go
14	觉得	juéde	to feel, to think
15	有意思	yǒuyìsi	interesting, fun

2c Puzzle It Out PROGRESS CHECK

Complete the exercises below to check your understanding of what you learned in Section 2. If you have questions, consult the Language Reference section.

Exercise 1 Read the Chinese sentences, then choose the best English translation.

1 那儿没有篮球场。

(a) You don't have a basketball court.

(b) There isn't a basketball court over there.

2 这儿有中文学校吗?

(a) Is there a Chinese school here?

(b) Does your school have Chinese classes?

3 我哥哥的学校有三个足球场。

(a) There are three soccer fields at my older brother's school.

(b) My older brother has three soccer balls.

Exercise 2 Complete the sentences by adding 是 or 很 .

1 她 ____ 喜欢打篮球。

2 她 ____ 我妹妹。

3 我觉得足球 ____ 有意思。

Language Reference

3 Using 有 to describe what can be found in an area

The word 有 can be used to express what a person has, but it can also be used to describe what can be found in a certain place.

1 A: 哪儿有篮球场(chǎng)?	Where is there a basketball court?
B: 我学校有篮球场(chǎng)。	There is a basketball court at my school.
2 A: 这儿(zhèr)有篮球场(chǎng)吗?	Is there a basketball court here?
B: 没有。这儿(zhèr)有足球场(chǎng)。	No, there is a soccer field here.

4 Description sentences with 很

In Chinese, the adjective, or description word, can act as the verb. The verb 是 is then left out, and the word 很 is usually added before the adjective. While 很 can be translated as "very" or "really," its meaning is not always that strong, especially in this kind of description.

1 我觉得(juéde)网球很有意思(yǒuyìsi)。	I think tennis is very interesting.
2 这个老师很好。	This teacher is very good.

2d Using the Language INTERPERSONAL

Find a partner and play the guessing game 你在哪儿? Pick one of the 小区 and keep your choice a secret. To win, you must correctly guess your partner's 小区 before your partner guesses yours. If you make an incorrect guess, you automatically lose! Follow these rules:

Start your turn by saying 你在哪儿?

Then, use 有 to ask your partner a question about his/her 小区.

After your partner answers the question, he/she will get a turn to ask you one.

Example:

A: 你在哪儿？那儿有篮球场吗？

B: 这儿没有篮球场。你在哪儿？那儿有中文学校吗？

网球场
篮球场
英文学校

A小区

足球场
中文学校
英文学校

B小区

中文学校
网球场
足球场

C小区

英文学校
中文学校
篮球场

D小区

Describing the location of activities

3a Language Model TARGET LANGUAGE INPUT

Your teacher will lead a discussion about the image below. Try to participate as much as you can. If there is anything you don't understand, let your teacher know.

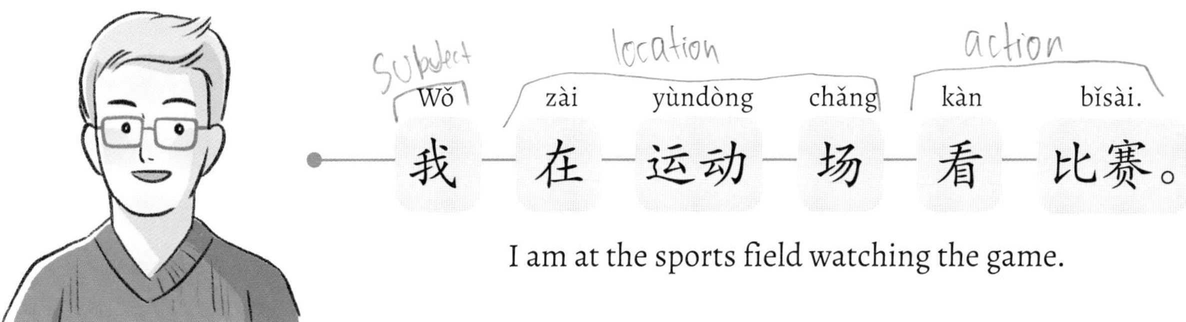

Wǒ zài yùndòng chǎng kàn bǐsài.
我在运动场看比赛。
I am at the sports field watching the game.

A sports field at a middle school in the city of Dalian

Audio

3b New Words in Conversation INTERPRETIVE

Listen to the audio and try to understand as much as you can of Leo and Maya's phone conversation. Then read the dialogue, using the pinyin text and vocabulary list to figure out unfamiliar words.

加油！加油！ — Jiā yóu! Jiā yóu!

你现在在哪儿? — Nǐ xiànzài zài nǎr?

我在足球馆! — Wǒ zài zúqiú guǎn!

你会踢足球吗? — Nǐ huì tī zúqiú ma?

我不太会。我不经常做运动。可是我经常在足球馆看比赛! — Wǒ bú tài huì. Wǒ bù jīngcháng zuò yùndòng. Kěshì wǒ jīngcháng zài zúqiú guǎn kàn bǐsài!

Comprehension Check

		T	F
1	Leo is at an indoor soccer field.	○	○
2	Leo can play soccer well.	○	○

Audio

Vocabulary

	Word	Pinyin	Meaning
16	加油	jiā yóu	Do your best! Go! (shouted to cheer players on, literally means "add fuel")
17	馆	guǎn	indoor court or field (for playing sports)
18	经常	jīngcháng	frequently, often
19	做	zuò	to do, to make
20	运动	yùndòng	sports, exercise
21	在	zài	at, in
22	比赛	bǐsài	game, match, competition

3c Puzzle It Out PROGRESS CHECK

Complete the exercise below to check your understanding of what you learned in Section 3. If you have questions, consult the Language Reference section.

Use the words in the list to complete the translation of each sentence. You may use some words more than once.

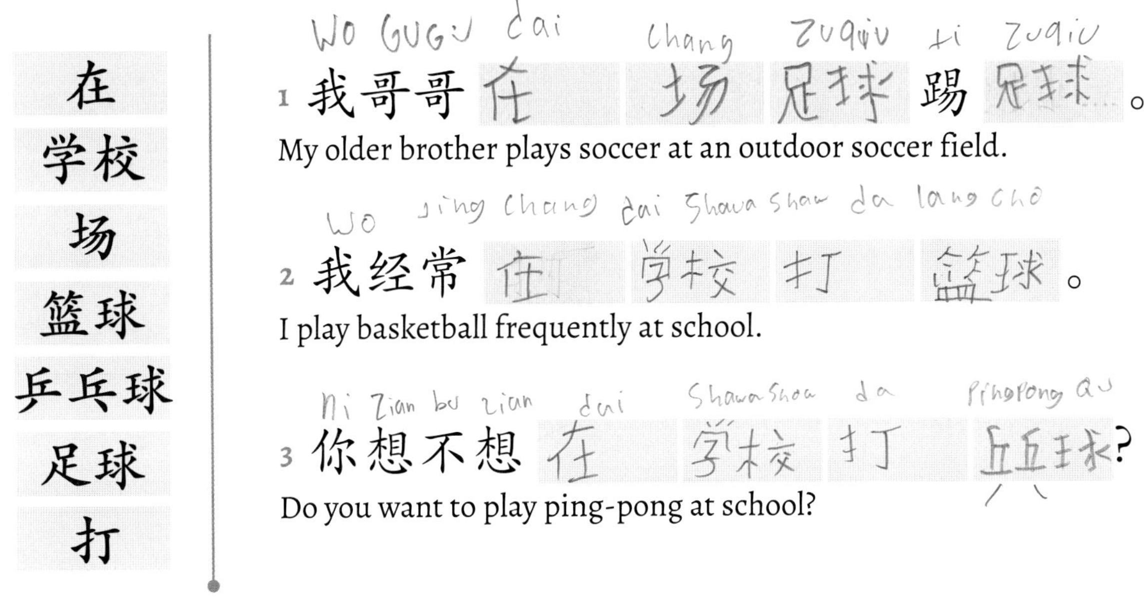

在

学校

场

篮球

乒乓球

足球

打

1 我哥哥 ______ ______ ______ 踢 ______。
My older brother plays soccer at an outdoor soccer field.

2 我经常 ______ ______ ______ ______。
I play basketball frequently at school.

3 你想不想 ______ ______ ______ ______？
Do you want to play ping-pong at school?

Language Reference

5 Using 在 to talk about where you do things

In Chinese, the word 在 is used to state where someone is doing something. In English, the location often comes at the end of the sentence. For example, "I play basketball at school." In Chinese, however, the location usually comes between the subject and the verb. It cannot be put at the end of the sentence. Unlike in English, the location phrase does not move when asking questions in Chinese.

	Location		Meaning
1 我	在学校	打篮球。	I play basketball at school.
2 你想	在家	看乒乓球比赛（bǐsài）吗？	Do you want to watch the ping-pong match at home?
3 你想	在哪儿	看乒乓球比赛（bǐsài）？	Where do you want to watch the ping-pong match?

TAKE NOTE!

经常 (jīngcháng) may appear before or after the location phrase. To emphasize the location of the activity, place 经常 (jīngcháng) before the location phrase.

我经常在学校打篮球。(jīngcháng) I play basketball frequently *at school.*

我在学校经常打篮球。(jīngcháng) I frequently *play basketball* at school.

Public parks are a favorite place for many urban Chinese to relax and enjoy their hobbies. In fine weather you can see people playing badminton, flying kites, or even line dancing! This man, photographed at the Temple of Heaven park in Beijing, is practicing calligraphy with water and a large brush. What kinds of activities are popular in your local parks? Are they similar to or different from the activities in Chinese parks?

3d Using the Language INTERPERSONAL

What do you and your classmates frequently do? In groups, brainstorm a list of sentences describing activities you frequently do and where you do them. Use the Word Bank below to help you. Compare your list with another group. Are there similarities or differences?

zuò gōngkè
1 做功课
do homework

kān dìdi
2 看弟弟
watch (babysit) younger brother

kān mèimei
3 看妹妹
watch (babysit) younger sister

zuò jiāwù
4 做家务
do household chores

dǎ yóuxì
5 打游戏
play video/computer games

tīng yīnyuè
6 听音乐
listen to music

What a Character!

The character 心 (xīn) means "heart." Characters that include this component often relate to thoughts or feelings. As a component, it often appears in the lower half of characters. 心 (xīn) looks like 忄 when it appears on the left side of a character.

Look at the characters below. Do they contain either form of 心 (xīn)?

1 您 2 情 3 很 4 想 5 快 6 说 7 急 8 忡

Put the Pieces Together!

A Reading and Listening INTERPRETIVE

Passage 1

DAMING, MARTIN, AND ISABELLA GO FOR A WALK TO EXPLORE THEIR NEW NEIGHBORHOOD.

7
你会踢足球吗？
看，那儿有一个足球场。

9
我不会踢足球……
我觉得踢足球也
没有意思……

10
乒乓球馆
你们看，乒乓球！
对，那是乒乓球馆。
我经常在那儿打乒乓球。

11

马丁，春月，
你们会打乒乓球吗？

我不会打乒乓球。

我也不太会打乒乓球……
可是我和马丁喜欢看乒乓球比赛。

MUSIC

12

你们现在想看
乒乓球比赛吗？

想！

Comprehension Check 

		T	F
1	Both Isabella and Martin like playing sports.	○	○
2	Isabella can play basketball and ping-pong well.	○	○
3	Isabella thinks basketball and soccer are boring.	○	○
4	Daming can play ping-pong.	○	○

Passage 2 Based on the sign below, answer the following questions.

1 If you wanted to play tennis, would you go to the left or to the right?

2 If you wanted to play basketball, would you go to the left or to the right?

3 Do you recognize any other words or characters on this sign?

Passage 3 Listen to the speaker talk about the sports he and his classmates play. Are the following statements true (T) or false (F)?

		T	F
1	The speaker frequently plays sports with his classmates at school.	○	○
2	All the students like playing basketball and soccer.	○	○
3	None of the students can play tennis or ping-pong.	○	○
4	The students don't want to play basketball this week because they want to play soccer.	○	○

B Speaking INTERPERSONAL

How sports-oriented are your classmates? In groups, discuss which sports you play, where you play them (for instance, at home, at school, or at a sports field), which sports you like to watch, and which sports you'd like to learn. Take notes on the responses of your group members to tell the class about your discussion.

Example:

A: 谁会踢足球?

B: 我不会踢足球，可是我喜欢看足球比赛。

C: 我会踢足球。我经常在学校踢足球。

A: 我想学踢足球。

C Final Project PRESENTATIONAL

Build a Community Sports Complex

Your town plans to build a new sports complex, or 体育馆 (tǐyù guǎn). You've been selected to be a part of the planning committee. What kinds of facilities would you include and why?

Step 1: Write four sentences describing some sports you like or can play.

Step 2: Imagine what the sports complex for your town would look like, and draw it. Check the Word Bank below for some extras you may want to include.

Step 3: Present your drawing to the class and tell them what facilities it includes.

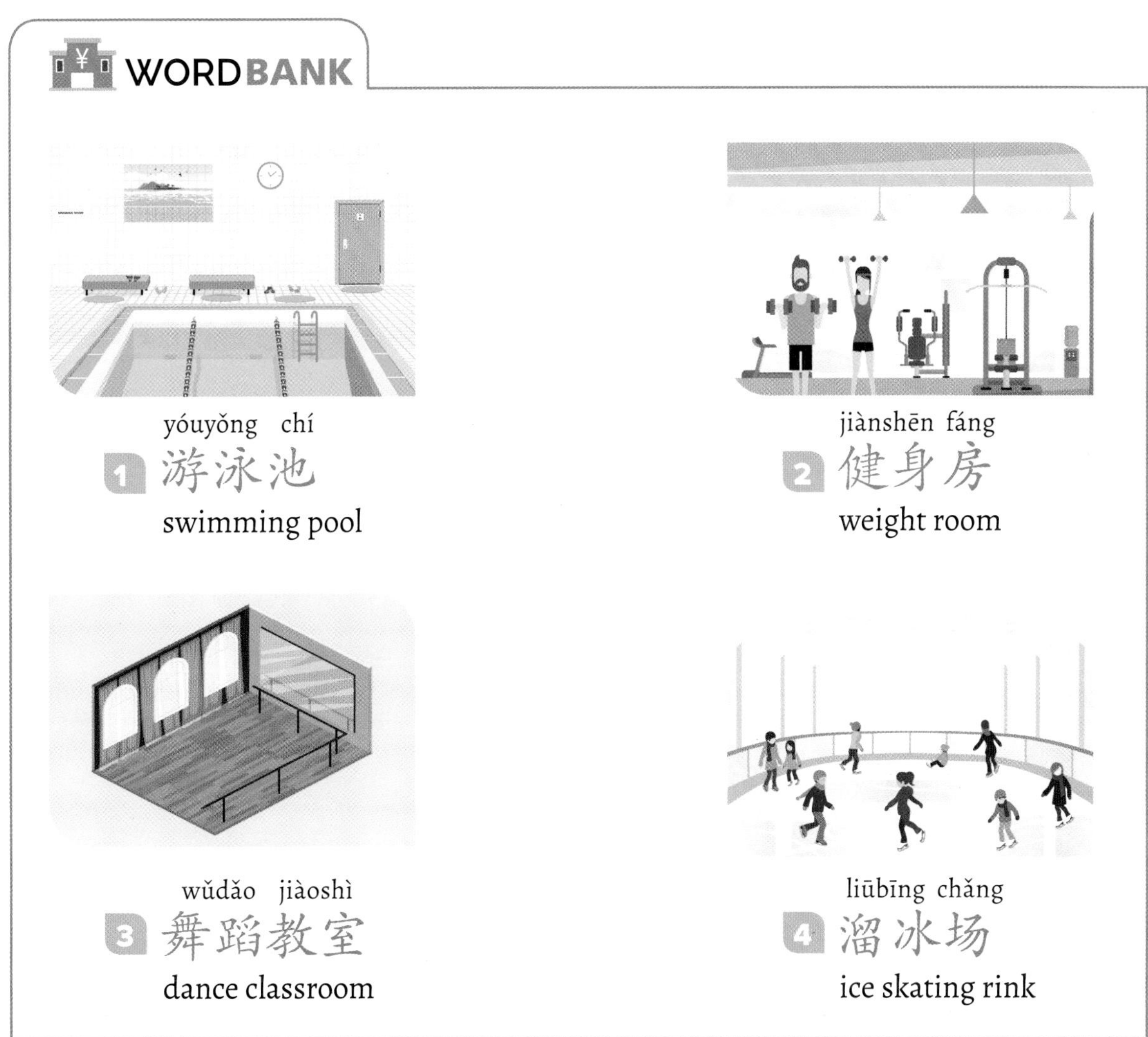

WORD BANK

1. yóuyǒng chí 游泳池 swimming pool
2. jiànshēn fáng 健身房 weight room
3. wǔdǎo jiàoshì 舞蹈教室 dance classroom
4. liūbīng chǎng 溜冰场 ice skating rink

Can-Do Goals

Talk with your teacher if you have questions or if you are not certain you can do the following tasks:

- Name some sports that are popular in China
- Discuss which sports you can play
- Say where you play sports
- Express whether or not you want to play a sport
- Understand the sports others can and want to play
- Ask if others want to play or watch sports

Cultural Knowledge

What did you learn about sports in China?

People play ping-pong along the Xi'an city wall.

Appreciating New Sounds

CHAPTER 6

第 dì 六 liù 课 kè

Emma: Let's open these boxes. This should be the last of our shipments from America.

Martin: Oh no! Look at my guitar!

Isabella: What happened?

Martin: The case got crushed, and now my guitar is ruined!

Isabella: It might not be easy to get a new guitar in Beijing...

Emma: Don't worry! Daming will be coming over soon for your Chinese lesson. We'll ask him for help.

Can-Do Goals

In this chapter, you will learn to:

- Recognize some traditional Chinese musical instruments and their sounds
- Understand when others talk about playing different kinds of instruments
- Say which instruments you play or want to learn to play
- Offer to teach someone to play an instrument, and say who teaches you
- Understand how the words 呢, 啊, and 吧 change the meaning or tone of a sentence

Chinese people are enthusiastic fans of different kinds of music. Many young people in China learn a musical instrument; popular choices include the piano, the violin, and the guitar. However, it is also common to choose a traditional Chinese instrument. For example, the 古筝 (gŭzhēng), shown above, is considered an easy instrument for beginners.

On a Different Note

If you've ever listened to Chinese music and thought it sounded exotic, it might be because of the scale. Most popular Western music uses a seven-note scale. However, most traditional Chinese instruments are tuned to a five-note scale.

And the Winner Is...

Music competition programs are popular in many countries, including China. Some shows feature professionals from countries around the world, while others search for the next great Chinese songwriter, and still others showcase aspiring young pop stars.

Online or Outdoors

The digital age has arrived for Chinese music lovers. One popular app, QQ Music, has over 250 million users! But when the weather is nice, many Chinese people head outside to listen to amateur musicians who play live in local parks. The photo here shows a trio playing guitar, saxophone, and 二胡 (èrhú) in Cuihu Park in the city of Kunming.

By the Numbers

China makes more pianos than any other country in the world and most are purchased by Chinese people.

Who buys the pianos made in China?

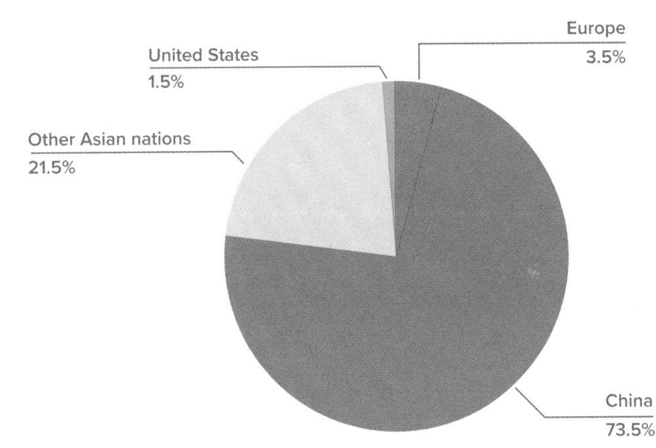

Source: Chinese Musical Instrument Association, 2010

REFLECT ON THE ESSENTIAL QUESTION

How does where you live affect what you do?

1. What kinds of music do you like?
2. When and where do you listen to music?
3. How did you (or would you) decide which instrument to learn to play?

Playing musical instruments

1a Language Model TARGET LANGUAGE INPUT

Your teacher will lead a discussion about the images below. Try to participate as much as you can. If there is anything you don't understand, let your teacher know.

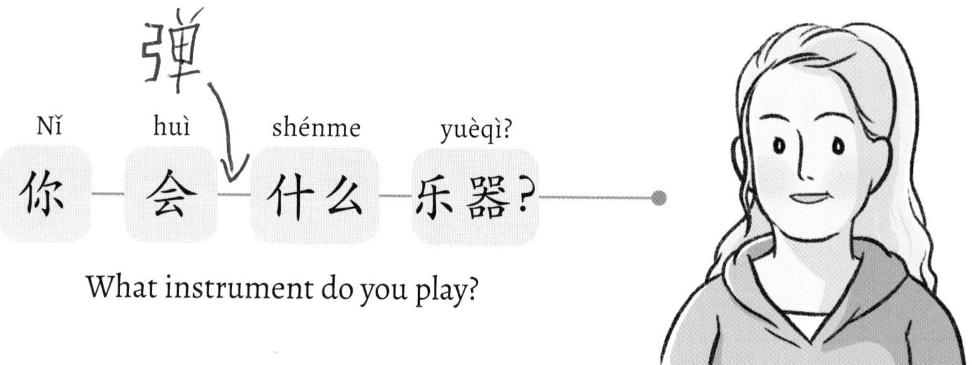
Nǐ huì shénme yuèqì?
你 会 什么 乐器?

What instrument do you play?

Audio

1

tán jítā
弹吉他
play guitar

2

tán gǔzhēng
弹古筝
play guzheng

3

chuī dízi
吹笛子
play flute

4

lā èrhú
拉二胡
play erhu

1b New Words in Conversation INTERPRETIVE

Listen to the audio and try to understand as much as you can. Then read the dialogue, using the pinyin text and vocabulary list to figure out unfamiliar words.

我会弹吉他。你们会什么乐器？ — Wǒ huì **tán jítā**. Nǐmen huì shénme **yuèqì**?

我会弹古筝，也会拉二胡。 — Wǒ huì **tán gǔzhēng**, yě huì **lā èrhú**.

我不会乐器。可是我很想学吹笛子。我觉得吹笛子很有意思。 — Wǒ bú huì **yuèqì**. Kěshì wǒ hěn xiǎng xué **chuī dízi**. Wǒ juéde **chuī dízi** hěn yǒuyìsi.

Comprehension Check

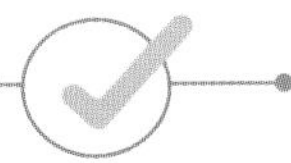

		T	F
1	Ellen can play the guitar.	○	○
2	Miko can play the guitar and also the guzheng.	○	○

Vocabulary

	Word	Pinyin	Meaning
1	弹	tán	to strum, to pluck, to play
2	吉他	jítā	guitar
3	乐器	yuèqì	musical instrument
4	古筝	gǔzhēng	guzheng
5	拉	lā	to pull, to play
6	二胡	èrhú	erhu
7	吹	chuī	to blow, to play
8	笛子	dízi	flute

1c Puzzle It Out PROGRESS CHECK

Complete the exercise below to check your understanding of what you learned in Section 1. If you have questions, consult the Language Reference section.

Choose the word from the list that best completes each sentence. You will not use all the words.

拉
吹
弹
吉他
二胡

1 我的哥哥会 弹 古筝。
2 我的爸爸会 拉 二胡。
3 我不会弹 吉他 。
4 你会不会 吹 笛子?

Language Reference

1 Chinese words for playing instruments

In English, the word "play" is used for many different kinds of instruments. In Chinese, however, different verbs are used to describe how various types of instruments are played.

吹 (chuī): to blow	黑管 (hēiguǎn)	clarinet
	萨克斯 (sàkèsī)	saxophone
弹 (tán): to strum, to pluck	钢琴 (gāngqín)	piano
	尤克里里 (yóukèlǐlǐ)	ukelele
拉 (lā): to pull	小提琴 (xiǎotíqín)	violin
	大提琴 (dàtíqín)	cello
打 : to hit	鼓 (gǔ)	drums

1d Using the Language INTERPERSONAL

Write three sentences in Chinese describing what you and your family members can do. Two statements should be true and one should be false. Read your sentences to a classmate who will try to guess which statement is false. If your partner identifies the false statement, you lose, but if your classmate picks one of the true statements, you win.

Student 1: A，我会踢足球。B，我的妈妈会弹吉他。
C，我的哥哥会打篮球。

Student 2: B 不对，你的妈妈不会弹吉他！

Student 1: 对！她不会弹吉他。OR 不对！她会弹吉他！

5Cs CONNECTIONS
COMMUNITIES
COMMUNICATION
CULTURES
COMPARISONS

Confucius, one of China's most influential thinkers, believed in the power of music. He encouraged his followers to study music, arguing that music is both enjoyable and beneficial. During Confucius's lifetime 2,500 years ago, the music scene was quite different. The philosopher never heard an erhu or a guzheng, but an ancient Chinese ensemble might have included flutes, drums, and bells.

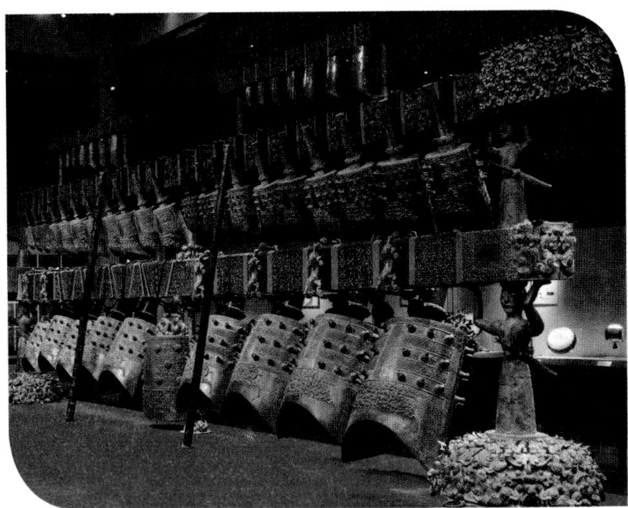

This instrument dates to the time period when Confucius was alive. What kind of instrument do you think it is?

Exclamations, suggestions, and questions

2a Language Model TARGET LANGUAGE INPUT

Your teacher will lead a discussion about the image below. Try to participate as much as you can. If there is anything you don't understand, let your teacher know.

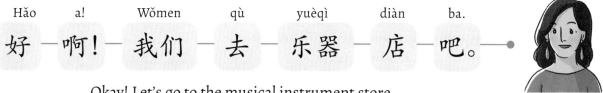

Māma, wǒ xiǎng mǎi jítā!
妈妈，我想买吉他！
Mom, I want to buy a guitar!

Hǎo a! Wǒmen qù yuèqì diàn ba.
好啊！我们去乐器店吧。
Okay! Let's go to the musical instrument store.

2b New Words in Conversation INTERPRETIVE

Audio

Listen to the audio and try to understand as much as you can. Then read the dialogue, using the pinyin text and vocabulary list to figure out unfamiliar words.

我想学弹吉他，也想学吹笛子。你呢？

Wǒ xiǎng xué tán jítā, yě xiǎng xué chuī dízi. Nǐ **ne**?

我想学拉二胡，可是我没有二胡。

Wǒ xiǎng xué lā èrhú, kěshì wǒ méiyǒu èrhú.

那个乐器店卖二胡。我们现在去买吧！

Nàge yuèqì **diàn mài** èrhú. Wǒmen xiànzài qù **mǎi ba**!

好啊！

Hǎo **a**!

Comprehension Check

		T	F
1	Owen wants to learn guitar and flute.	○	○
2	Ellen also wants to learn guitar.	○	○

Vocabulary

Audio

	Word	Pinyin	Meaning
9	呢	ne	(word added at the end of a sentence to ask a follow-up question or to ask a question back to someone)
10	店	diàn	store, shop
11	卖	mài	to sell
12	买	mǎi	to buy
13	吧	ba	(word added at the end of a sentence to make a suggestion or to soften the tone)
14	啊	a	(word added at the end of a sentence to add emphasis or excitement)

2c Puzzle It Out PROGRESS CHECK

Complete the exercise below to check your understanding of what you learned in Section 2. If you have questions, consult the Language Reference section.

Use the words in the list to complete the translation of each sentence below. Use each word once.

吧
啊
呢

1 我想买乐器。你 呢 ?
I want to buy an instrument. What about you?

2 我们去那个中国乐器店 吧 !
Let's go to that Chinese instrument store!

3 你很会拉二胡 啊 !
You're really good at playing erhu!

Language Reference

2 Using 啊, 吧, and 呢

In addition to 吗, there are a number of other words in Chinese that do not have a meaning of their own. These words change the meaning or tone of the whole sentence.

	How to use	Examples
啊	Use to show excitement, surprise, or even annoyance. The exact meaning depends on the speaker's tone of voice.	1 好啊 (a)！ Okay! 2 对啊 (a)！ That's right!
吧	Use to make the tone more polite and to turn a command into a suggestion.	3 我们去那儿吧 (ba)！ Let's go there! 4 你学古筝吧 (ba)。 You should learn guzheng.
呢	Use to ask a question back to someone or to ask a follow-up question.	5 你呢 (ne)？ And you? 6 他呢 (ne)？ What about him?

2d Using the Language INTERPERSONAL

For this game, you will be assigned two musical instruments. The first will be a musical instrument that you own and can sell. The second will be a musical instrument that you want to buy. Take a look at the chart below: You can only buy and sell the instruments that are next to the one you own. For example, if you have a flute, your first purchase must be either a drum or a clarinet. Your task is to buy and sell different musical instruments until you can finally buy the one you want.

A: 我卖笛子。你呢?

B: 我卖二胡。你买我的二胡吧!

A: 我不买。

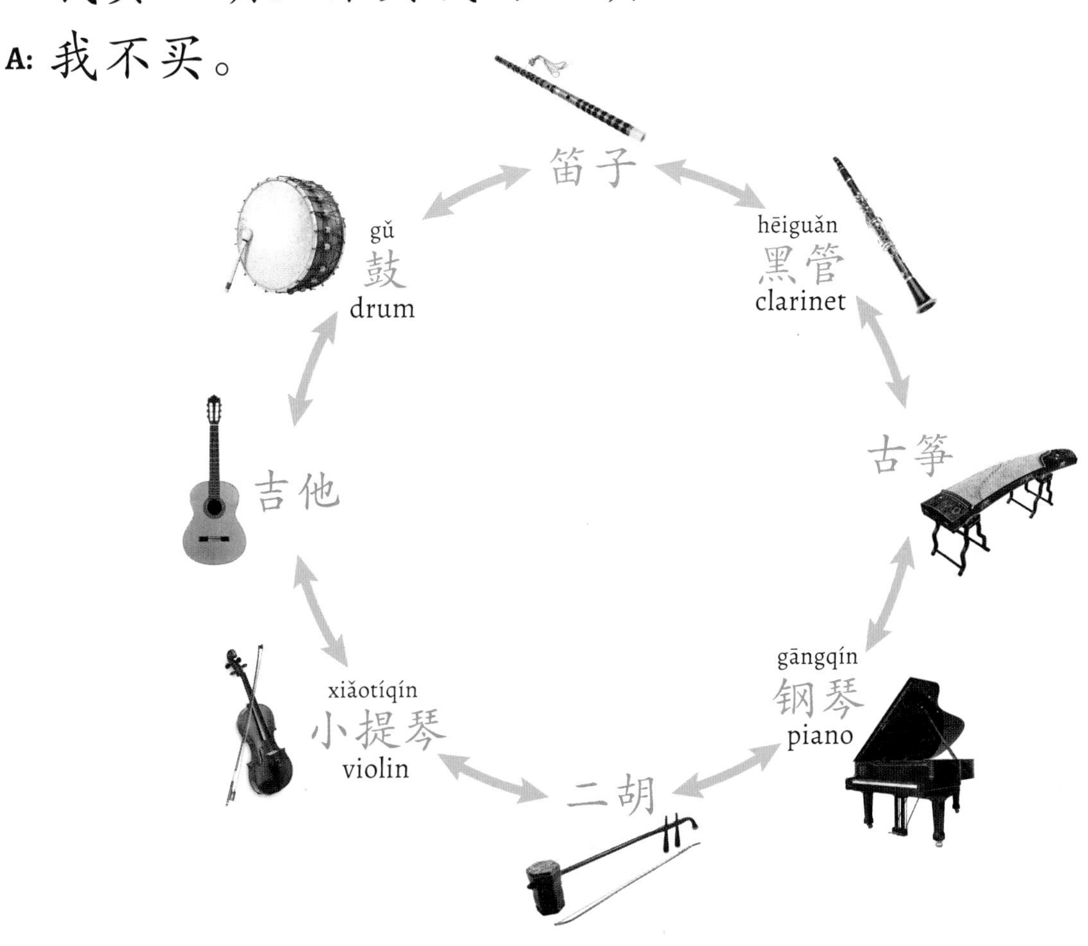

LANGUAGE CHALLENGE

Make a list of your favorite instruments. Then use a dictionary to look up how to say them in Chinese. Don't forget to figure out which verb goes with each instrument!

Teaching and learning musical instruments

3a Language Model TARGET LANGUAGE INPUT

Your teacher will lead a discussion about the image below. Try to participate as much as you can. If there is anything you don't understand, let your teacher know.

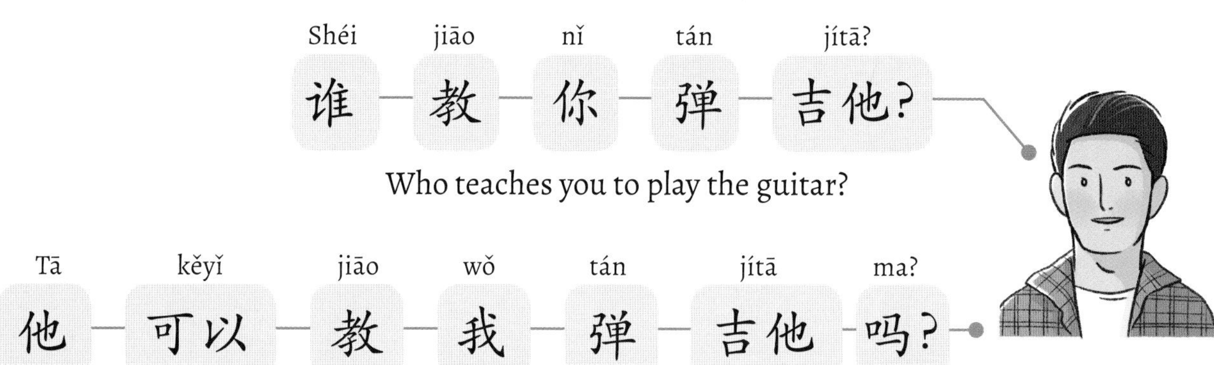

Shéi jiāo nǐ tán jítā?
谁 教 你 弹 吉他?
Who teaches you to play the guitar?
Tā kěyǐ jiāo wǒ tán jítā ma?
他 可以 教 我 弹 吉他 吗?

Can he teach me to play the guitar?

3b New Words in Conversation INTERPRETIVE

Listen to the audio and try to understand as much as you can. Then read the dialogue, using the pinyin text and vocabulary list to figure out unfamiliar words.

李老师，我姐姐是你的学生。她经常在家拉二胡。

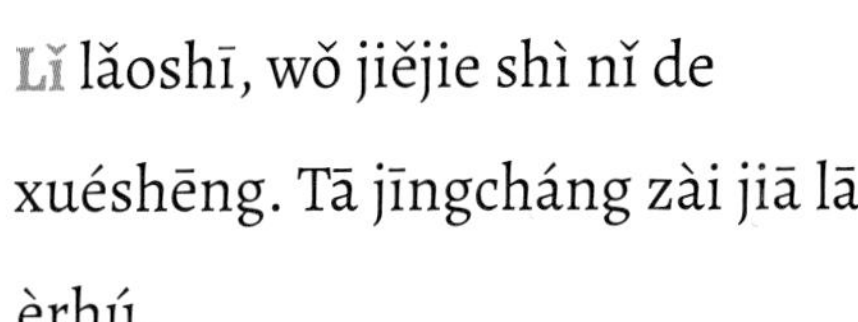

Lǐ lǎoshī, wǒ jiějie shì nǐ de xuéshēng. Tā jīngcháng zài jiā lā èrhú.

是吗？你也喜欢听中国音乐吗？

Shì ma? Nǐ yě xǐhuan tīng Zhōngguó yīnyuè ma?

很喜欢！我也想学二胡。你可以教我拉二胡吗？

Hěn xǐhuan! Wǒ yě xiǎng xué èrhú. Nǐ kěyǐ jiāo wǒ lā èrhú ma?

可以啊！

Kěyǐ a!

谢谢！

Xièxie!

Comprehension Check

		T	F
1	Mr. Li teaches Ellen's older sister erhu.	○	○
2	Ellen does not like Chinese music.	○	○

Vocabulary

Audio

	Word	Pinyin	Meaning
15	听	tīng	to listen to, to hear
16	音乐	yīnyuè	music
17	可以	kěyǐ	can, could, may
18	教	jiāo	to teach
19	谢谢	xièxie	thank you, thanks
	李	Lǐ	Li (surname, sometimes spelled Lee)

3c Puzzle It Out PROGRESS CHECK

Complete the exercises below to check your understanding of what you learned in Section 3. If you have questions, consult the Language Reference section.

Exercise 1 Rearrange the Chinese words and phrases in each row to translate the English sentences.

1 你 | 教 | 古筝？ | 弹 | 谁
Who teaches you to play the guzheng?

2 古筝。 | 我 | 李老师 | 教 | 弹
Mr. Li teaches me to play the guzheng.

3 也 | 教 | 人 | 李老师 | 二胡吗？ | 拉
Does Mr. Li also teach people to play the erhu?

4 李老师 | 二胡。 | 对， | 也 | 人 | 教 | 拉
Yes, Mr. Li also teaches people to play the erhu.

Exercise 2 Complete the sentences by adding 会 or 可以. Use the English translation to help you.

1 你 ____ 弹古筝吗？
Can you play the guzheng?

2 我 ____ 买这个吉他吗？
May I buy this guitar?

3 妈妈，我 ____ 看电视吗？
Mom, can I watch TV?

4 我不 ____ 乐器。
I can't play a musical instrument.

5 你 ____ 教我妹妹吗？
Could you teach my younger sister?

3 Using the verb 教

Like the English verb "to teach," 教 (jiāo) can be used to say that a person teaches someone about something or teaches someone to do something.

	Someone	教	someone	something
1	Lǐ 李老师 Mr. Li	jiāo 教 teaches	我们 us	中文。 Chinese.
2	我 I	jiāo 教 teach	他 him	拉二胡。 to play the erhu.

4 会 vs. 可以

While 会 is used to talk about things that you learned how to do, 可以 (kěyǐ) is used to talk about things you can do because you have the permission or the circumstances allow. In English, we might use the words can, could, or may in the place of 可以 (kěyǐ).

1 我不会打篮球。

I can't play basketball (because I don't know how).

2 妈妈，我现在可以(kěyǐ)去打篮球吗？

Mom, can I go play basketball now?

3 你会弹吉他吗？

Can you play the guitar?

4 你不可以(kěyǐ)在这儿弹吉他！

You may not play the guitar here! (Situation: You're in the library.)

3d Using the Language INTERPERSONAL

In this activity, you and your classmates will be assigned to one of the four teacher profiles below. Each teacher can teach two skills and wants to learn two more. Read the profiles carefully! Your task is to interview your classmates to find out who can teach you the things you want to learn.

A: 我想学吉他。你可以教我弹吉他吗？

B: 我不会弹吉他……我想学笛子。你可以教我吗？

A: 可以啊！

A老师
会：二胡，篮球
想学：足球，古筝

B老师
会：乒乓球，吉他，足球
想学：二胡，网球

C老师
会：笛子，网球
想学：吉他，篮球

D老师
会：网球，古筝
想学：乒乓球，笛子

What a Character!

bā
巴

1 2 3 4

This component can give you an idea of how to say characters it is a part of. Many characters with this component are pronounced "ba." This component is generally found on the bottom or right side of a character.

Guess how to say the characters below:

1 把 (third tone)
2 爸 (fourth tone)
3 芭 (first tone)
4 粑 (first tone)
5 疤 (first tone)
6 靶 (third tone)

CHAPTER 6

Put the Pieces Together!

A Reading and Listening INTERPRETIVE

Passage 1

DAMING IS AT MARTIN AND ISABELLA'S HOME FOR A CHINESE LESSON WHEN EMMA ASKS FOR HELP WITH AN ERRAND.

乐器店
这不是吉他店。
吉他店在那儿。
这是中国乐器店。

你们听，
这是什么乐器？

这是二胡。
李老师在这儿卖乐器，
也在这儿教二胡。

我想学二胡！
妈妈，我可以买二胡吗？
可以啊。
谢谢！

我想学这个乐器。
这是什么乐器，大明？
这是古筝。

11

妈妈，我可以买古筝吗？
可以啊！
谢谢！

12
李老师教马丁拉二胡，
马丁教大明弹吉他。
大明教你弹古筝，好吗？

Comprehension Check

		T	F
1	Martin can play the guitar.	○	○
2	Isabella does not play an instrument.	○	○
3	Isabella does not like to listen to music.	○	○
4	Daming can play the guitar.	○	○
5	Martin decides to learn to play the erhu.	○	○

Passage 2 This music school offers summer lessons. Name at least two instruments that are taught at the school.

音乐之声艺术学校
钢琴、小提琴、架子鼓、尤克里里
古筝、二胡、笛子、琵琶、扬琴
联系人：李老师
报名电话：010-6234XXXX

Passage 3 Listen to the two short conversations. Answer the questions on a separate piece of paper.

Audio

Conversation 1  

1 Which instrument does Maya know how to play?

2 Which instrument does she want to study?

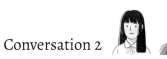

Conversation 2  

3 Which instruments does Miko know how to play?

4 Which instrument will she teach?

B Speaking INTERPERSONAL

Work with your group to create a survey to ask the following questions:

1 Do you want to learn a musical instrument?

2 What instrument would you like to learn?

3 Can you already play an instrument?

4 What instrument can you play?

Use this survey to interview your classmates. Work with the other students in your group to create a plan that matches the students who want to study an instrument to one of the students who already plays that instrument. Make a list of which students will teach other students. Write down which students do not have a teacher because none of their classmates know how to play the instrument they want to learn.

C Final Project PRESENTATIONAL

Getting Into the Music Business

You've decided to open a business for people in your community who want to take up a new instrument. Decide what kind of business you will open and make a flyer to try to convince your classmates to come to your business! How many customers can you find?

Example:

A: 这是我的乐器店。你们买古筝吧！ [Student A shows the flyer to students B and C.]

B: 好啊！

C: 我不想买古筝。你卖不卖二胡？

A: 我也卖二胡！

Can-Do Goals

Talk with your teacher if you have questions or if you are not certain you can do the following tasks.

- Recognize some traditional Chinese musical instruments and their sounds
- Understand when others talk about playing different kinds of instruments
- Say which instruments you play or want to learn to play
- Offer to teach someone to play an instrument, and say who teaches you
- Understand how the words 呢, 啊, and 吧 change the meaning or tone of a sentence

Cultural Knowledge

What did you learn about music in China?

A man plays the erhu in a park in the city of Tianjin.

CELEBRATING SPECIAL OCCASIONS

In Unit 3, you will learn how Chinese people celebrate birthdays and other special days. By the end of the unit, you will also know how to talk about past and future events.

Unit 3

第 dì 三 sān 单 dān 元 yuán

A dragon dance is part of the Spring Festival celebration in Vancouver, Canada's Chinatown.

Essential Question

What makes a day special?

CHAPTER 7
Do You Have Plans?

While making plans for the weekend, Isabella and Martin remember that a special day is coming!

CHAPTER 8
Shopping for the Perfect Gift

Daming helps Isabella and Martin shop for the perfect present.

CHAPTER 9
A Birthday Dinner

It's Emma's birthday, and Isabella and Martin have ordered her a spectacular birthday dinner!

UNIT 3 PROJECT

At the end of the unit, you will imagine that your class is planning a party for an exchange student's birthday. To plan the party, you will:

- Read about what the exchange student likes and when he has free time
- Choose a gift, a date for the party, and some food to order
- Present your birthday party plan to the class

Do You Have Plans?

CHAPTER 7

第 dì
七 qī
课 kè

Isabella: Hey Martin, want to go to a movie later?

Martin: I can't. I'm going to swim practice soon.

Isabella: Didn't you have swim practice on Monday?

Martin: No, that was my guitar lesson.

Isabella: We just moved here, and you already have so much going on! I guess we'll have to go to the movies some other time...

Can-Do Goals

In this chapter, you will learn to:

- State the date and the day of the week of an upcoming activity
- Understand numbers larger than ten
- Discuss when you are free
- Ask and answer questions about birthdays
- Talk about buying a gift based on someone's interests

CULTURE CONNECTION

qìnghè

庆贺

Celebrations

When celebrating a holiday or a birthday, it's important to plan in advance to make sure the occasion receives the attention it deserves.

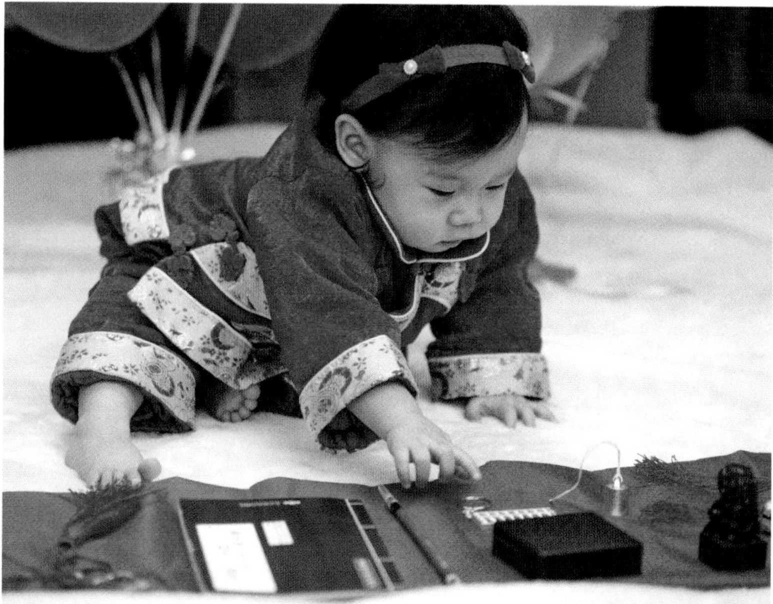

Happy First Birthday

When a child turns one, many Chinese parents invite relatives to a party to watch the baby do a "birthday grab," or 抓周 (zhuāzhōu). To prepare, the parents spread objects associated with different occupations in front of the baby. The object the baby grabs first is thought to predict his or her future career.

The Traditional Chinese Calendar

Many Chinese holidays fall on different dates from year to year. This is because the dates for these holidays are still calculated using the traditional Chinese calendar, which is often called the lunar calendar because it is partially based on the phases of the moon.

七月 July

S	M	T	W	T	F	S
	1 廿九	2 三十	3 六月	4 初二	5 初三	6 初四
7 小暑	8 初六	9 初七	10 初八	11 初九	12 初十	13 十一
14 十二	15 十三	16 十四	17 十五	18 十六	19 十七	20 十八
21 十九	22 二十	23 大暑	24 廿二	25 廿三	26 廿四	27 廿五
28 廿六	29 廿七	30 廿八	31 廿九			

Chinese calendars often include the date according to the traditional calendar.

Chinese New Year

春节 (Chūnjié), often called Chinese New Year or Spring Festival, marks the first day of the new year according to the traditional calendar. 春节 is the most important holiday for many Chinese people. With much of the population traveling to visit family during the holiday season, train tickets often sell out quickly, so buying them as soon as they become available is a must.

Travelers throng Hangzhou's train station during the Spring Festival travel rush.

Trips Taken During the Spring Festival Travel Period (approximate)

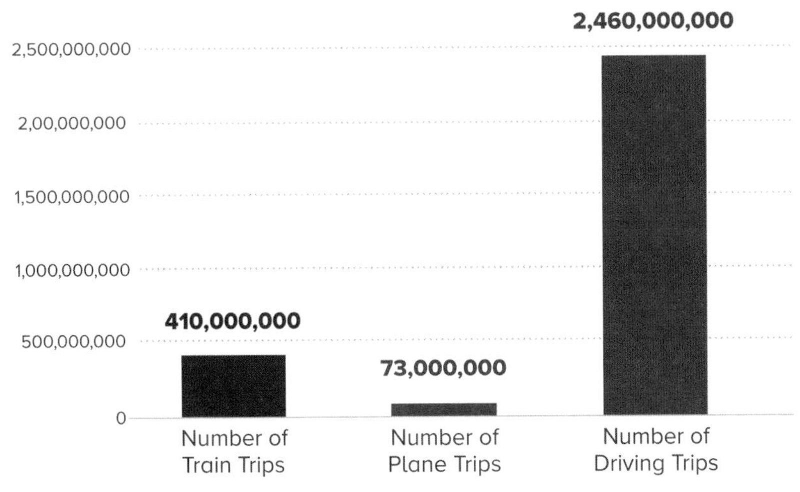

Source: Xinhua News Agency, 2019

By the Numbers

Travel in China over the New Year holiday period results in the largest annual human migration on Earth.

REFLECT ON THE ESSENTIAL QUESTION

How do you prepare for a special day?

1. Do you celebrate birthdays? If so, how do you celebrate them?
2. Do you celebrate any holidays that fall on different dates each year? How are the dates determined?
3. How do you and your family get ready for important holidays?

Scheduling an activity

1a Language Model TARGET LANGUAGE INPUT

Your teacher will lead a discussion about the image below. Try to participate as much as you can. If there is anything you don't understand, let your teacher know.

Nǐ jīntiān yǒu kòng ma?
你今天有空吗?

Do you have free time today?

Wǒmen qù kàn diànyǐng ba?
我们去看电影吧?

Let's go see a movie, okay?

1b New Words in Conversation INTERPRETIVE

Listen to the audio and try to understand as much as you can. Then read the dialogue, using the pinyin text and vocabulary list to figure out unfamiliar words.

	今天是星期几?	Jīntiān shì xīngqī jǐ?
	今天是星期五。	Jīntiān shì xīngqīwǔ.
	我们去看电影吧?	Wǒmen qù kàn diànyǐng ba?
	我今天没有空。我们明天去，好吗?	Wǒ jīntiān méiyǒu kòng. Wǒmen míngtiān qù, hǎo ma?
	可是明天我没有空……我们后天去看电影，好不好?	Kěshì míngtiān wǒ méiyǒu kòng... Wǒmen hòutiān qù kàn diànyǐng, hǎo bù hǎo?
	好!	Hǎo !

Comprehension Check 

		T	F
1	Maya asks Ellen to go to the movies with her.	○	○
2	Ellen does not have free time today.	○	○
3	Ellen suggests that they go see the movie the day after tomorrow instead.	○	○
4	This conversation takes place on Thursday.	○	○
5	Maya and Ellen ultimately decide to see the movie on Friday.	○	○

Audio

Vocabulary

	Word	Pinyin	Meaning
1	今天	jīntiān	today
2	星期五	xīngqīwǔ	Friday
3	电影	diànyǐng	movie, motion picture
4	有空	yǒu kòng	to have free time, to be free
5	明天	míngtiān	tomorrow
6	后天	hòutiān	the day after tomorrow

1c Puzzle It Out PROGRESS CHECK

Complete the exercises below to check your understanding of what you learned in Section 1. If you have questions, consult the Language Reference section.

Fill in the blanks to complete the translations below.

1 后天 是星期 一 。
The day after tomorrow is Monday.

2 他星期 ____ 没有 ____ 空。
He doesn't have free time on Sunday.

3 你想星期 几 去 看 电影？
Which day of the week do you want to go see a movie?

4 明天 是 星期五 吗？
Is tomorrow Friday?

Language Reference

1 Days of the week

The days of the week in Chinese follow the simple pattern: 星期 + number. Sunday is the only day of the week that does not follow this pattern.

星期一 Monday	星期二 Tuesday	星期三 Wednesday	星期四 Thursday	星期五 Friday
星期六 Saturday		星期天 or 星期日* Sunday		

*星期日 (xīngqīrì) is used more often in writing, while 星期天 (xīngqītiān) is used more often in conversation—but both words mean Sunday.

Add 几 at the end of 星期 to ask questions about the day of the week.

1 今天（是）星期一。(jīntiān) → 今天（是）星期几？(jīntiān)

Today is Monday. → What day of the week is it today?

2 她星期天去踢足球。(tiān) → 她星期几去踢足球？

She will go play soccer on Sunday. → Which day of the week will she go play soccer?

What a Character!

日 (rì)

1 日 2 日 3 日 4 日

The character 日 (rì) means "sun" or "day." As a component, it is often (but not always) found on the left side of the character.

Can you find 日 (rì) in each character below? What do you notice about the meanings of these characters?

1 时 time
2 早 morning
3 晒 shine
4 昨 yesterday
5 晚 night
6 晴 sunny

1d Using the Language INTERPERSONAL

Step 1: Imagine that your family has moved to Beijing. The school year is about to start, and it's time to pick your after-school activities. On a separate sheet of paper, write a schedule for your school week. In your schedule, you should have one afternoon with free time. For the remaining four days, pick one activity per day from the After-School Activity Schedule.

After-School Activity Schedule:

星期一	星期二	星期三	星期四	星期五
学中文 拉二胡	弹吉他 打乒乓球	打篮球 弹吉他	弹古筝 打网球	踢足球 吹笛子

Sample Student Schedule:

星期一	星期二	星期三	星期四	星期五
拉二胡	有空	打篮球	弹古筝	踢足球

Step 2: A new movie has just come out, and you want to find some classmates who can go with you. Go around the classroom and search for classmates who are free on the same day that you are. If your classmate asks you about a day when you have an activity scheduled, be sure to tell him or her what you will be doing that day.

Example:

A: 你星期五有空吗?

B: 没有空。我星期五想去踢足球。

Students in the city of Zhongshan

Talking about birthdays

2a Language Model TARGET LANGUAGE INPUT

Your teacher will lead a discussion about the image below. Try to participate as much as you can. If there is anything you don't understand, let your teacher know.

Nǐ de shēngrì shì jǐ yuè jǐ hào?

你的生日是几月几号?

What month and day is your birthday?

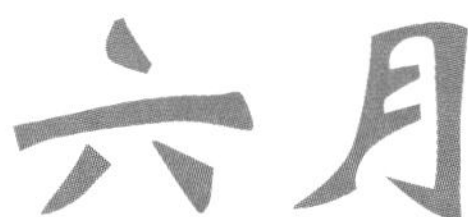

第 25 周

星期一 16

星期二 17

星期三 18

星期四 19

星期五 20

星期六 21  Miko 的生日

星期天 22

Audio

2b New Words in Conversation INTERPRETIVE

Listen to the audio and try to understand as much as you can. Then read the dialogue, using the pinyin text and vocabulary list to figure out unfamiliar words.

你的生日是几月几号？ — Nǐ de shēngrì shì jǐ yuè jǐ hào?

我的生日是六月二十一号。 — Wǒ de shēngrì shì liùyuè èrshíyī hào.

六月二十一号是下个星期五！ — Liùyuè èrshíyī hào shì xià ge xīngqīwǔ!

不是，是下个星期六。 — Bú shì, shì xià ge xīngqīliù.

我们下个周末去看电影吧？ — Wǒmen xià ge zhōumò qù kàn diànyǐng ba?

好啊！ — Hǎo a!

Comprehension Check

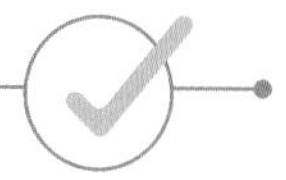

		T	F
1	Sanjay asks Miko when her birthday is.	○	○
2	Miko's birthday is on June 21st.	○	○
3	Miko's birthday is this Thursday.	○	○
4	Sanjay suggests that they go play basketball next weekend.	○	○

Vocabulary

	Word	Pinyin	Meaning
7	生日	shēngrì	birthday
8	月	yuè	month, moon
9	号	hào	day of the month
10	六月	liùyuè	June
11	二十一	èrshíyī	twenty-one
12	下个	xià ge	next
13	周末	zhōumò	weekend

2c Puzzle It Out PROGRESS CHECK

Complete the exercise below to check your understanding of what you learned in Section 2. If you have questions, consult the Language Reference section.

Use the words and phrases in the list to complete the translation of the dialogue.

几号
二十一
几月
十二
月
号

A: 你弟弟的生日是 ______ ______ ?
When is your younger brother's birthday?

B: 我弟弟的生日是 ______ ______ ______ ______ 。
My younger brother's birthday is December 21st.

2 Numbers 11-99

Once you know the numbers one through ten in Chinese, you have the tools to say all the numbers up to 99!

For numbers 11 to 19, start with ten and follow it with a second digit. For example, the number 11 can be directly translated as "ten one" (十一).

Stating the numbers for 20 and higher requires a little simple math. The Chinese word for 20 translates as "two tens" (二十). To continue counting up, just add the final digit. For example, 21 is "two ten one" (二十一). This pattern continues all the way through 99.

	Number of tens (if more than 1)	Ten	Single digit (1-9)	
For numbers 11-19		十	六	十六 → sixteen
For multiples of 10	四	十		四十 → forty
For other numbers above 20	四	十	六	四十六 → forty-six

3 Giving specific dates

The Chinese word for each month is simply the number plus the word 月 (yuè).

January	一月	May	五月	September	九月
February	二月	June	六月	October	十月
March	三月	July	七月	November	十一月
April	四月	August	八月	December	十二月

The word 号 (hào) placed after a number indicates a specific day of the month. 几 comes before 月 (yuè) and 号 (hào) in questions about dates.

shēngrì yuè hào
1 **Q:** 你的生日是几月几号? — When is your birthday? (What is the date of your birthday?)

shēngrì yuè hào
A: 我的生日是五月七号。 — My birthday is May 7th.

hào
2 **Q:** 今天（是）几号? — What is today's date?

hào
A: 今天是八号。 — Today is the 8th.

Are you able to recite this tricky tongue twister? Try to get the tones right, too!

四是四，十是十。
十四是十四，四十是四十，
四十四是四十四。
四不是十，十也不是四。
十四不是四十，四十也不是十四，
是不是?

2d Using the Language INTERPERSONAL

Create a class birthday calendar, like the one shown below, by asking your classmates when their birthdays are. Remember to include your teacher!

我们的生日

一月	二月	三月	四月	五月	六月
七月	**八月**	**九月**	**十月**	**十一月**	**十二月**

In both English and Chinese, there can be formal and informal ways of saying the same thing. For example, in English, "child" and "kid" have the same meaning, but "child" is used in more formal settings. In Chinese, there is more than one way to say "week." 星期 means week, but so does the more formal word 周 (zhōu). Knowing that 周 (zhōu) means week, try to guess the meaning of the character 末 (mò) in 周末 (zhōumò).

Reacting to new information

3a Language Model TARGET LANGUAGE INPUT

Your teacher will lead a discussion about the image below. Try to participate as much as you can. If there is anything you don't understand, let your teacher know.

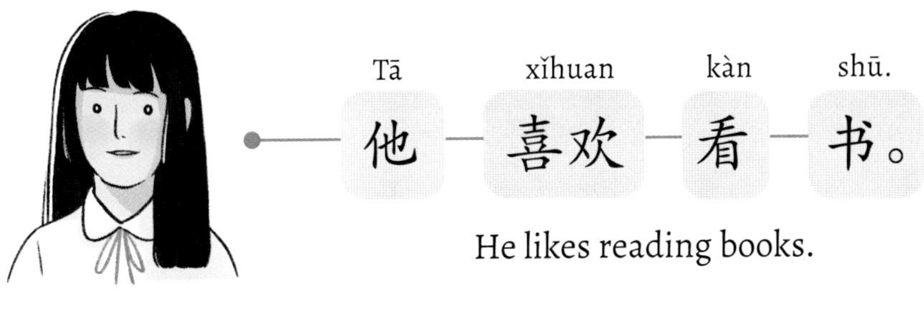

He likes reading books.

Nà wǒmen mǎi zhège lǐwù ba?
那我们买这个礼物吧?

In that case, shall we buy this gift?

3b New Words in Conversation INTERPRETIVE

Listen to the audio and try to understand as much as you can. Then read the dialogue, using the pinyin text and vocabulary list to figure out unfamiliar words.

这个星期天是春月的生日，可是我不知道买什么礼物。

Zhège xīngqītiān shì Chūnyuè de shēngrì, kěshì wǒ bù zhīdào mǎi shénme lǐwù.

那你问马丁吧。他一定知道。

Nà nǐ wèn Mǎdīng ba. Tā yídìng zhīdào.

好主意！我明天去问他。

Hǎo zhǔyi! Wǒ míngtiān qù wèn tā.

Comprehension Check

		T	F
1	Isabella's birthday is next Saturday.	○	○
2	Leo doesn't know what gift to buy.	○	○
3	Maya suggests that Leo ask Isabella's mom what to buy.	○	○
4	Leo thinks that Maya's idea is a good one.	○	○

Vocabulary

	Word	Pinyin	Meaning
14	礼物	lǐwù	gift
15	那	nà	in that case, then, so
16	问	wèn	to ask (a question)
17	一定	yídìng	certainly, definitely
18	主意	zhǔyi	idea

3c Puzzle It Out PROGRESS CHECK

Complete the exercise below to check your understanding of what you learned in Section 3. If you have questions, consult the Language Reference section.

Use the words in the list to complete the translation of the dialogue.

去	A: 你 ____ 想 ____ ____ 足球吗？ Do you want to go play soccer tomorrow?
那	B: 我不喜欢踢足球。我喜欢 ____ 。 I don't like to play soccer. I like to play basketball.
吧	A: ____ 我们明天去打篮球 ____ ？ In that case, let's go play basketball tomorrow, okay?
明天	
打篮球	
踢	

Language Reference

4 Responding to new information with 那

In addition to meaning "that," 那 (nà) can also mean "in that case." When used in this way, 那 (nà) links the information from the sentence or phrase before it with the conclusion or suggestion that comes after.

New Information	那	Conclusion/Suggestion
1 A: 明天是我的生日。 A: Tomorrow is my birthday.	B: 那 (nà) B: In that case,	我们去看电影吧？ let's go see a movie, okay?
2 A: 我今天没有空，可是我明天有空。 A: I don't have time today, but I do have time tomorrow.	B: 那 (nà) B: In that case,	我们明天去打网球吧？ let's go play tennis tomorrow, okay?
3 A: 她很喜欢听音乐。 A: She likes listening to music.	B: 那 (nà) B: In that case,	她一定 (yídìng) 喜欢这个礼物 (lǐwù)！ she will certainly like this present!

3d Using the Language INTERPERSONAL

You and your classmates want to get a gift to thank your teacher for all of his or her hard work.

Step 1: Prepare one question that asks about your teacher's interests. When the teacher calls on you, ask your question and write down your teacher's response.

Step 2: Listen as your classmates ask their questions. On a separate piece of paper, keep notes on your teacher's responses.

Step 3: In small groups, discuss the gift options pictured here. Based on your teacher's responses, which gifts shown here would your teacher like? Suggest a gift for the class to buy.

Example:

林老师很喜欢拉二胡。那我们买这个吧!

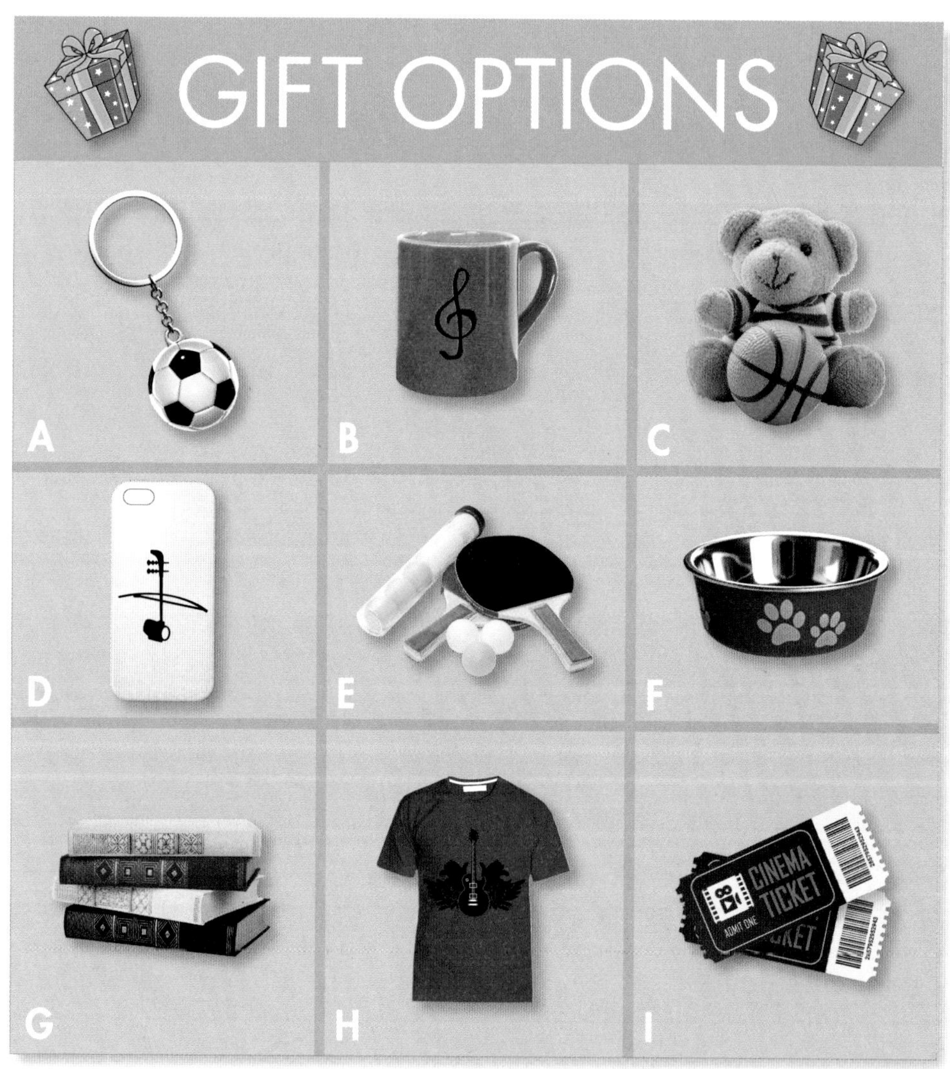

Put the Pieces Together!

A Reading and Listening INTERPRETIVE

Audio

Passage 1

ISABELLA AND MARTIN TALK ABOUT THEIR SCHEDULES AND REALIZE THAT AN IMPORTANT DAY IS COMING UP SOON.

5
今天是星期三，
七月九号。
6
下个星期五是
七月……十八号！

7
妈妈的生日！

8
我们这个周末
去买生日礼物吧！

9
好啊，可是我
不知道去哪儿
买礼物……
我也不知道……

10

大明是北京人，
他一定知道去哪儿买礼物。
我们明天问他吧。

好主意！

11

那我们后天去看电影吧？

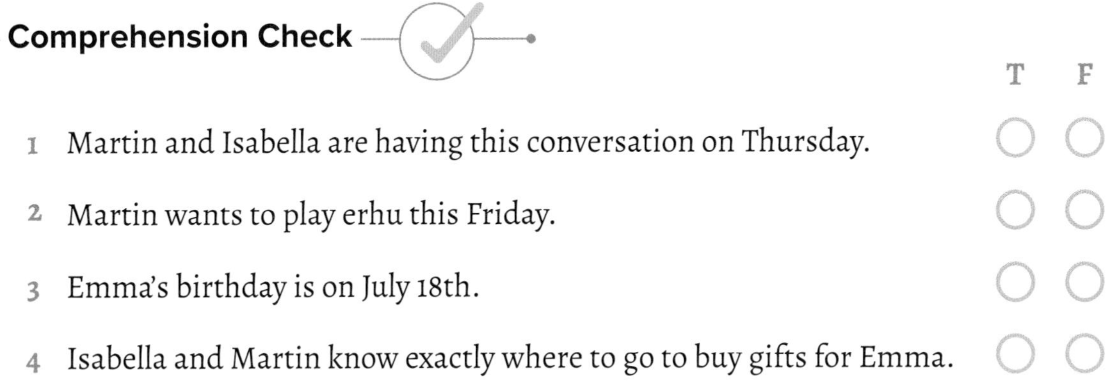

Comprehension Check

		T	F
1	Martin and Isabella are having this conversation on Thursday.	○	○
2	Martin wants to play erhu this Friday.	○	○
3	Emma's birthday is on July 18th.	○	○
4	Isabella and Martin know exactly where to go to buy gifts for Emma.	○	○

Passage 2 This year, your class plans to decorate the classroom for your Chinese teacher's birthday. Which decoration would be the most appropriate?

Bonus: Can you guess which decoration is for Chinese New Year?

Passage 3 Listen to Leo talk to his mom about living a healthier lifestyle. Are the following statements true (T) or false (F)?

Audio

		T	F
1	Leo has already exercised today.	○	○
2	Leo plans to exercise tomorrow.	○	○
3	Leo will exercise with Martin the day after tomorrow.	○	○
4	Leo says he will exercise this weekend.	○	○

B Speaking PRESENTATIONAL

In pairs or groups, create a skit in which a group of friends discuss their plans for the next few days. Where are they going, and what do they plan to do? Refer to the images and keywords for ideas for your skit. Practice your skit and then perform it for your class.

Keywords: 想，这儿，那儿，去 + action，有意思，觉得，可是，那，吧，今天，明天，后天，星期六

A

B

C

D

C Final Project PRESENTATIONAL

Comic Strip

Draw and write a comic strip that has three or more panels.

Step 1: Decide on characters and a setting.

Step 2: Pick one of the suggested titles below, or get creative and come up with your own!

爸爸的生日是几月几号？
我这个星期没有空……
我有一个好主意！
他／她一定很喜欢这个礼物！

Step 3: Draft the dialogue of the comic and then have your teacher check it.

Step 4: Plan out how much space you need for your comic. Draw a rough sketch.

Step 5: Create a final draft of your comic strip based on your teacher's feedback.

Can-Do Goals

Talk with your teacher if you have questions or if you are not certain you can do the following tasks:

- State the date and the day of the week of an upcoming activity
- Understand numbers larger than ten
- Discuss when you are free
- Ask and answer questions about birthdays
- Talk about buying a gift based on someone's interests

Cultural Knowledge

What did you learn about some Chinese celebrations?

People in Beijing celebrating the Chinese New Year by performing a lion dance.

Shopping for the Perfect Gift

CHAPTER 8

第 dì 八 bā 课 kè

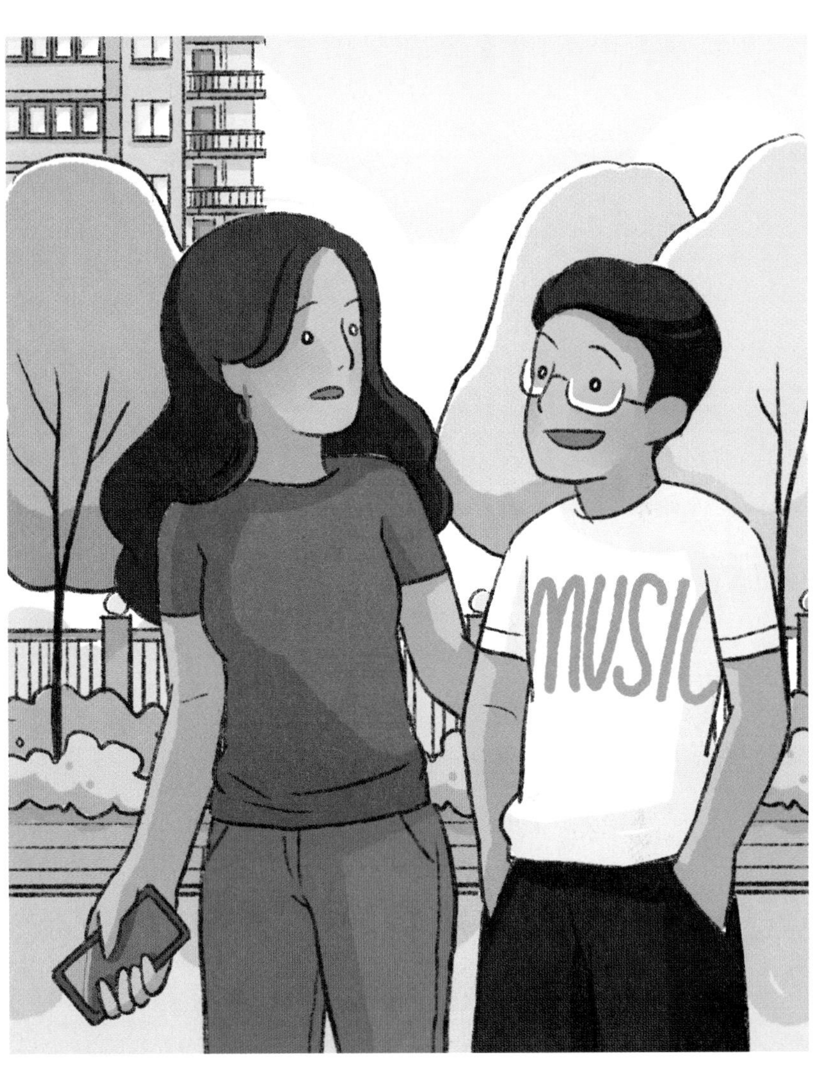

Isabella: I can't believe we almost forgot Mom's birthday!

Martin: It's coming up soon, but I don't know what to get her.

Isabella: Me neither! She's so hard to shop for.

Martin: I guess we'll figure it out when we get to the store...?

Isabella: I'll call Daming now to see if he has time to help us.

Can-Do Goals

In this chapter, you will learn to:

- Understand when others describe what they are going to do
- Talk about when you are busy and when you plan to do certain activities
- Use appropriate greetings for phone conversations
- Agree or disagree with someone
- Discuss purchasing a gift for someone
- Give simple descriptions of books and clothes

sòng lǐwù

送礼物

Giving Gifts

In China, as in many cultures, giving gifts is a way of marking a special occasion like a holiday, a birthday, or even a dinner at a friend's home. Giving a gift to someone is also a way to show care and respect.

Think Local

特产 (tè chǎn), or local specialty products, are popular gifts in China because they can be hard to get outside of the region where they are made. Examples of 特产 include authentic Dragonwell tea from Hangzhou and rose cakes, such as the one shown here, from Yunnan Province.

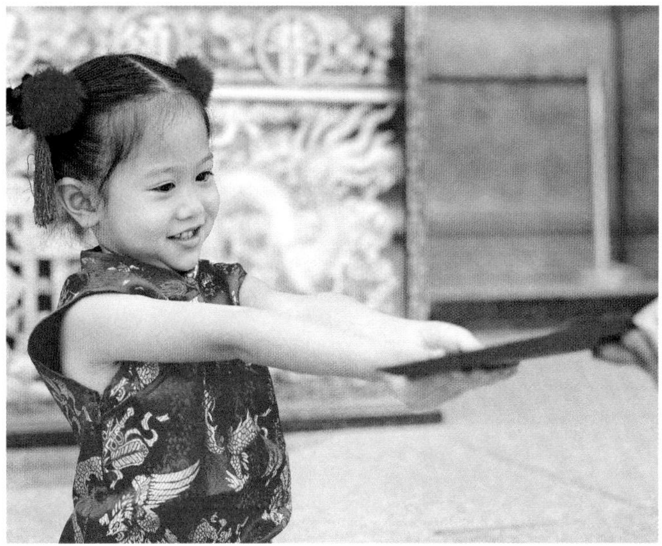

Red Envelopes

In China 红包 (hóngbāo), or red envelopes filled with money, are a traditional gift on many special days, including Spring Festival and weddings. The envelope's red color symbolizes good luck and happiness. The money inside the 红包 should be crisp and new. As a result, holiday preparations often include a trip to the bank to withdraw fresh bills. When giving or receiving a gift, including 红包, it is considered polite to hold it with both hands.

By the Numbers

In recent years, it has become increasingly popular to use digital red envelopes to give money electronically, as shown in this image. During the busiest six days of Spring Festival in 2019, Chinese people sent and received over 823 million digital 红包 on WeChat, a social media site.

REFLECT ON THE ESSENTIAL QUESTION

How do you prepare for a special day?

1. When do you give gifts? Are certain kinds of gifts expected for specific occasions?
2. When looking for a gift for someone, how do you decide what to get? Are there particular things that are considered special gifts in your culture? If so, why?
3. How do you prepare to give a gift to someone? Are wrapping and presenting the gift important?

Times of day

1a Language Model TARGET LANGUAGE INPUT

Your teacher will lead a discussion about the images below. Try to participate as much as you can. If there is anything you don't understand, let your teacher know.

Wǒ xiàwǔ yào qù tī zúqiú.
我下午要去踢足球。

I am going to go play soccer this afternoon.

Nǐ xiàwǔ yǒu shì ma?
你下午有事吗？

Do you have something to do this afternoon?

3
zhōngwǔ
中午
noon

2
shàngwǔ
上午
morning
(before noon)

4
xiàwǔ
下午
afternoon

1
zǎoshàng
早上
early morning
(until about 9:00 a.m.)

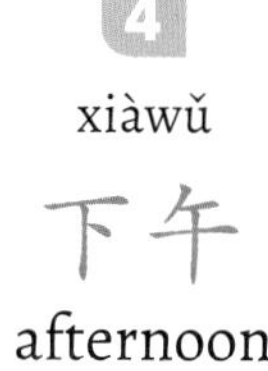

5
wǎnshàng
晚上
night, evening

1b New Words in Conversation INTERPRETIVE

Listen to the audio and try to understand as much as you can. Then read the dialogue, using the pinyin text and vocabulary list to figure out unfamiliar words.

喂，Maya，早上好！ — Wéi, Maya, zǎoshàng hǎo!

早上好，Owen！ — Zǎoshàng hǎo, Owen!

我和春月今天想去看电影。你想去吗？ — Wǒ hé Chūnyuè jīntiān xiǎng qù kàn diànyǐng. Nǐ xiǎng qù ma?

我今天下午要去踢足球，晚上也有事……你们明天晚上有空吗？ — Wǒ jīntiān xiàwǔ yào qù tī zúqiú, wǎnshàng yě yǒu shì... Nǐmen míngtiān wǎnshàng yǒu kòng ma?

有！那我们明天晚上去看电影吧！ — Yǒu! Nà wǒmen míngtiān wǎnshàng qù kàn diànyǐng ba!

好，明天见！ — Hǎo, míngtiān jiàn!

明天见！ — Míngtiān jiàn!

Comprehension Check

		T	F
1	Owen is talking to Maya on the phone.	○	○
2	This conversation takes place in the afternoon.	○	○
3	Owen wants to play soccer with Maya today.	○	○
4	Maya is busy this afternoon and evening.	○	○
5	Owen and Maya agree to meet up tomorrow night.	○	○

Vocabulary

Audio

	Word	Pinyin	Meaning
1	喂	wéi	hello (over the phone)
2	早上	zǎoshàng	early morning (until about 9:00 a.m.)
3	下午	xiàwǔ	afternoon
4	要	yào	to be going to (do something), to want (something; to do something)
5	晚上	wǎnshàng	night, evening
6	事	shì	thing, matter, something to do
7	见	jiàn	to meet with, to see
8	中午	zhōngwǔ	noon
9	上午	shàngwǔ	morning (before noon)

1c Puzzle It Out PROGRESS CHECK

Complete the exercise below to check your understanding of what you learned in Section 1. If you have questions, consult the Language Reference section.

Which word should be added to the following sentences? Choose 要, 想, or either 要 or 想.

	要	想	Either 要 or 想
1 我明天晚上 ______ 去做运动。 I'm going to go exercise tomorrow night.	○	○	○
2 我 ______ 看这个电影。 I want to watch this movie.	○	○	○
3 我 ______ 那本书。 I want that book.	○	○	○
4 我 ______ 买一只宠物。 I want to buy a pet.	○	○	○

Language Reference

1 Meanings and uses of 要

要 (yào) is a very common word that has a number of different meanings.

Definition 1 要 = going to (do something)

Note that 要 (yào) is left out when saying that someone is *not* going to do something.

1 她今天早上要去打乒乓球。(zǎoshàng yào) She is going to go play ping-pong this morning.

2 她今天早上不去打乒乓球。(zǎoshàng) She is not going to go play ping-pong this morning.

Definition 2 要 = to want (to do something)

This meaning of 要 (yào) is very similar to 想, but 要 (yào) shows more certainty. A speaker will usually use 要 (yào) if he or she has a plan in place or is ready to act. 想 shows the feeling of wanting to do something, even if the speaker doesn't know if or when he or she will be able to do that thing. When saying that someone does *not* want to do something, 想 is used more often than 要 (yào). Also, words like 很 and 不太 can only be used with 想, not with 要.

3 我要看电视。(yào) I want to watch TV. (Or: I am going to watch TV.)

4 我想看电视。 I want to (would like to) watch TV. (The tone is less certain than the tone in example 3.)

5 我不想看电视。 I don't want to watch TV.

Definition 3 要 = to want (something)

For this meaning of 要 (yào), the negative form is 不要 (bú yào).

6 我要这个！谢谢！(yào) I want this! Thank you!

7 我不要这个，我要那个。(yào, yào) I don't want this; I want that.

2 Time + 见

Adding 见 (jiàn) after a time word means "See you (at that time)!" 再见 follows the same pattern. 再 means "again," so 再见 literally means "See you again!"

Time	见	Meaning
1 下午 (xiàwǔ)	见! (jiàn)	See you this afternoon!
2 明天晚上 (wǎnshàng)	见! (jiàn)	See you tomorrow night!

1d Using the Language INTERPERSONAL

Do you keep your weekends open, or do you schedule many activities? What about your classmates?

Step 1: On a separate piece of paper, write out your schedule for the mornings, afternoons, and evenings for the coming weekend. Write 有事 if you have activities scheduled but don't know how to say them in Chinese. Write 没有事 or 有空 if you have no activities planned for that time.

Step 2: In groups, ask your classmates about their weekend plans and take notes. Are there any days or times when everyone has things planned or when everyone is free?

Step 3: Tell the class when your groupmates have free time and when they have plans. Listen as other groups report their schedules. Which days or times are most people busy? Which days or times are most people free? Are there any class-wide trends?

When you see someone early in the day, you might say "good morning" or just "morning." Similarly, Chinese people sometimes greet each other by simply saying 早 or may use the longer greeting 早上好.

Shopping choices

2a Language Model TARGET LANGUAGE INPUT

Your teacher will lead a discussion about the images below. Try to participate as much as you can. If there is anything you don't understand, let your teacher know.

Zhè běn shū hěn jiǎndān,
这本书很简单，
érqiě bú tài guì.
而且不太贵。

This book is very simple and also not too expensive.

1 jiǎndān 简单 simple

2 nán 难 difficult

3 piányi 便宜 cheap, inexpensive

4 guì 贵 expensive

Audio

2b New Words in Conversation INTERPRETIVE

Listen to the audio and try to understand as much as you can. Then read the dialogue, using the pinyin text and vocabulary list to figure out unfamiliar words.

我想买这**本**书。这**本**书很**便宜**。

Wǒ xiǎng mǎi zhè **běn** shū. Zhè **běn** shū hěn **piányi**.

可是这**本**书很**难**……看，那**本**书很**简单**，**而且**不太**贵**。

Kěshì zhè **běn** shū hěn **nán**... Kàn, nà **běn** shū hěn **jiǎndān**, **érqiě** bú tài **guì**.

那我要那**本**书。你呢？

Nà wǒ yào nà **běn** shū. Nǐ ne?

我今天不想买书。

Wǒ jīntiān bù xiǎng mǎi shū.

Comprehension Check

		T	F
1	The book Miko initially wants to buy is expensive.	○	○
2	Leo says that the first book Miko wants to buy is boring.	○	○
3	Leo points out a different book that is simple and also not too expensive.	○	○
4	Miko will likely buy the book that Leo points out to her.	○	○

Vocabulary

Audio

	Word	Pinyin	Meaning
10	本	běn	(measure word for books)
11	便宜	piányi	cheap, inexpensive
12	难	nán	difficult
13	简单	jiǎndān	simple
14	而且	érqiě	and also
15	贵	guì	expensive

2c Puzzle It Out PROGRESS CHECK

Complete the exercise below to check your understanding of what you learned in Section 2. If you have questions, consult the Language Reference section.

Can 而且 be used in the following sentences? Choose Yes or No.

		Yes	No
1	这本书很简单，________ 很贵。	○	○
2	那本书很有意思，________ 很便宜。	○	○

Language Reference

3 Adding more description with 而且

Like the English phrase "and also," 而且 (érqiě) is used to add more similar or supporting information. 而且 (érqiě) is not used to give different or contrasting descriptions.

		Description 1 (positive)	而且	Description 2 (positive)
1	这本(běn)中文书 This Chinese book	很有意思 is very interesting	而且(érqiě) and also	不太贵(guì)。 not too expensive.

		Description 1 (negative)	而且	Description 2 (negative)
2	这本(běn)英文书 This English book	很难(nán)， is very difficult	而且(érqiě) and also	很贵(guì)。 very expensive.

What a Character!

chuò 辶

The character component 辶 (chuò) is often called zǒuzhīdǐ. This component usually appears on the left side of a character. Many characters with this component have something to do with walking or movement.

Which of the following characters contain 辶 (chuò)?

1 送 2 说 3 远 4 近 5 起 6 迎 7 进 8 得

2d Using the Language INTERPERSONAL

Imagine that your Chinese teacher is building a classroom library and would like to hear your opinions.

Step 1: Read the comments and ratings from the book reviews that follow.

Step 2: In pairs, talk about whether you like or don't like each of the books shown below. Give two reasons why you like or don't like each book. Do you both like the same books? Your teacher will ask about your opinions. Be prepared to share both your partner's and your own.

Example:

我喜欢这本书。这本书很有意思，而且不太难。

Reader Reviews

☆☆☆☆★

简单 —— 难

便宜 —— 贵

有意思 —— 没有意思

happy_reader: 这本书很简单！我和我的朋友都喜欢这本书。

Reader Reviews

☆☆☆☆★

简单 —— 难

便宜 —— 贵

有意思 —— 没有意思

Readtome_04: 这本书很有意思，可是我觉得这本书很难。

Reader Reviews

☆☆☆☆☆

简单 —— 难

便宜 —— 贵

有意思 —— 没有意思

Intellireader_2002: 这本书很有意思。

Reader Reviews

☆☆★★★

简单 —— 难

便宜 —— 贵

有意思 —— 没有意思

Too_tired22: 难！而且没有意思……

D

Buying clothes

3a Language Model TARGET LANGUAGE INPUT

Your teacher will lead a discussion about the image below. Try to participate as much as you can. If there is anything you don't understand, let your teacher know.

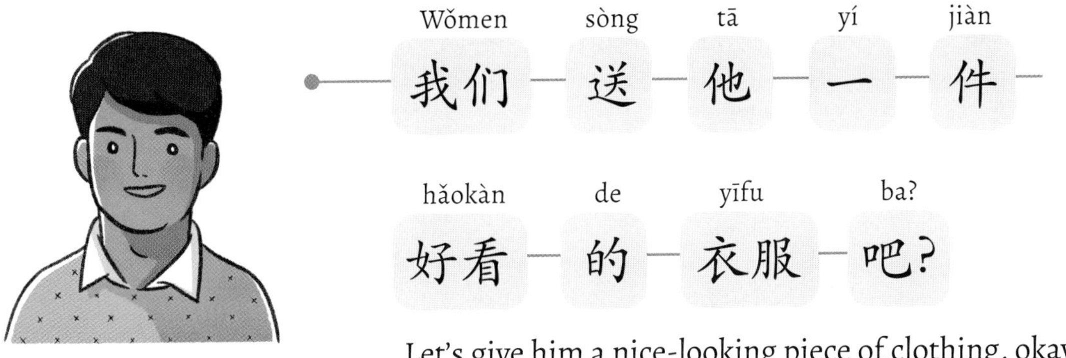

Wǒmen sòng tā yí jiàn
我们 送 他 一 件
hǎokàn de yīfu ba?
好看 的 衣服 吧?

Let's give him a nice-looking piece of clothing, okay?

yīfu

衣服

clothing

Audio

3b New Words in Conversation INTERPRETIVE

Listen to the audio and try to understand as much as you can. Then read the dialogue, using the pinyin text and vocabulary list to figure out unfamiliar words.

这件衣服很好看！我们送 Owen 这件衣服吧？

Zhè jiàn yīfu hěn hǎokàn! Wǒmen sòng Owen zhè jiàn yīfu ba?

可是我觉得这件衣服很贵。我们送他一件便宜的衣服吧？

Kěshì wǒ juéde zhè jiàn yīfu hěn guì. Wǒmen sòng tā yí jiàn piányi de yīfu ba?

好！那件衣服不贵，而且颜色很好看。我们送他那件衣服吧？

Hǎo! Nà jiàn yīfu bú guì, érqiě yánsè hěn hǎokàn. Wǒmen sòng tā nà jiàn yīfu ba?

好，我同意！

Hǎo, wǒ tóngyì!

Comprehension Check

		T	F
1	Sanjay suggests giving Owen a nice-looking piece of clothing.	○	○
2	Leo says that he thinks the clothing Sanjay suggested is not nice-looking.	○	○
3	Leo suggests that they give Owen something more expensive.	○	○
4	The clothing that Sanjay and Leo agree to give Owen is a nice color, but it's expensive.	○	○

Vocabulary

	Word	Pinyin	Meaning
16	件	jiàn	(measure word for clothing)
17	衣服	yīfu	clothing
18	好看	hǎokàn	good-looking, nice-looking (used for people and things)
19	送	sòng	to give (a gift)
20	颜色	yánsè	color
21	同意	tóngyì	to agree

3c Puzzle It Out PROGRESS CHECK

Complete the exercise below to check your understanding of what you learned in Section 3. If you have questions, consult the Language Reference section.

Make correct sentences by rearranging the words and phrases in each row.

1 礼物。| 喜欢 | 他 | 很贵 | 的

2 的 | 想买 | 一本 | 她 | 书。| 简单

3 朋友 | 他的 | 一件 | 衣服。| 想买 | 好看 | 的

4 有意思 | 要去看 | 一个 | 我明天 | 电影。| 的

4 Using 的 in descriptions

In English, we put adjectives (description words) right in front of the nouns being described. But in Chinese, 的 is used to link the description to the thing being described.

		Description words	的	Noun Being Described	Meaning
1	jiàn 一件	便宜	的	yīfu 衣服	an inexpensive piece of clothing
2	三本	有意思	的	书	three interesting books
3	那个	很贵	的	乐器	that very expensive musical instrument

This chart shows the names of the three primary colors in Chinese. Use a dictionary to look up how to say the other colors.

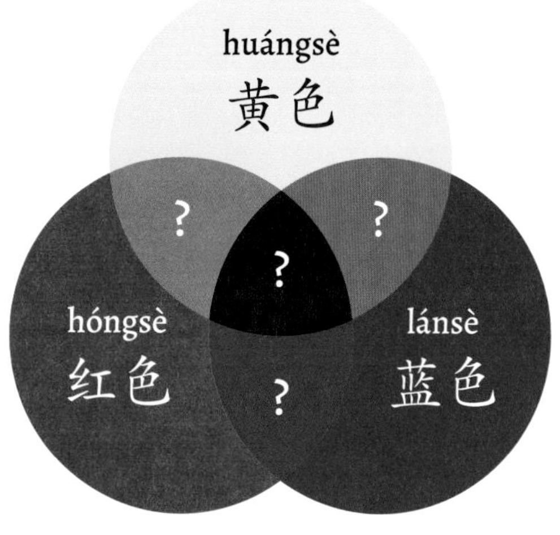

3d Using the Language INTERPERSONAL

Many middle and high schools in China have uniforms. Below are images showing different styles of uniforms that Chinese students might wear. If your school decided to choose a uniform, which one would you want the school to buy?

Step 1: Look at the images closely and choose your favorite uniform. Jot down at least two reasons for your selection.

Step 2: In groups, discuss the uniform options. Suggest one of the uniforms and explain the reasons why you like that option. How many of your groupmates agree with you? Take notes on the reasons they give for their preferences.

Example:

A: 这件衣服很好看。我们买这件吧?

B: 我同意！这个颜色的衣服很好看。

C: 我不同意。我不太喜欢这个颜色……

A middle school student from Jiangxi Province poses for the camera.

Students in Hebei Province prepare to exercise.

Hebei Province students participate in a group exercise routine.

High school students wait to cross the road in Hong Kong.

Put the Pieces Together!

A Reading and Listening INTERPRETIVE

Passage 1

ISABELLA AND MARTIN ASK DAMING TO HELP THEM FIND A BIRTHDAY GIFT FOR THEIR MOM.

1
喂，大明，早上好！下个星期五是我妈妈的生日。我和马丁要去买礼物。
MUSIC

2
可是，我们不知道去哪儿买礼物……你知道吗？

3
知道啊！我今天早上和中午有事……你们下午有空吗？
有！那我们下午见吧？

4
好，下午见！
谢谢！

6
你们看，这件衣服很好看！
妈妈很喜欢这个颜色。

7
我们送她这件衣服吧？
我不同意，我觉得这件
衣服不好看，而且很贵……

8
那中文书呢？
书很便宜。
对，妈妈要学中文。

9

10
我觉得这本书很有意思，
而且很便宜。我们送妈妈
这本书吧？
我不同意，
我觉得这本书很难……

11

那春月送妈妈
一件好看的衣服。

13

好主意，我同意！

我也同意！

Comprehension Check 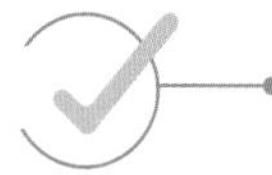

		T	F
1	Daming agrees to meet up with Martin and Isabella tomorrow morning.	○	○
2	Isabella wants to give her mom a nice-looking piece of clothing.	○	○
3	Martin agrees that the piece of clothing is nice-looking, but thinks it is very expensive.	○	○
4	In the end, Martin and Isabella decide they will both give their mother a Chinese book.	○	○

Passage 2 You are shopping for souvenirs on the streets of Beijing and see a store with a display of fridge magnets. The words in the red circles advertise a deal. What is the deal? Which magnets would you buy?

Passage 3 Listen to Miko and Sanjay's phone conversation and answer the following questions.

1 When is Owen's birthday?

(a) the day after tomorrow

(b) next Friday

(c) March 21st

2 What does Miko want to get for Owen's birthday?

(a) an inexpensive piece of clothing

(b) a nice-looking piece of clothing

(c) a book

3 When do Sanjay and Miko agree to go shopping?

(a) this morning

(b) tomorrow afternoon

(c) tomorrow night

B Speaking INTERPERSONAL

During your spring break, a local store, Huanhuan's (欢欢的小店), is celebrating its anniversary with a multi-day sales event. You have just $10 to spend. Check out Huanhuan's "Deal of the Day" flyer and tell your partner what days and times you want to go there. Point to the items you want to buy and give your reasons for wanting them, referring to the Word Bank below for ideas. Then listen to your partner's shopping plans and take notes so that you can tell the class about what your partner plans to buy.

Example:

A: 你星期几去欢欢的小店？

B: 我星期五上午和星期天下午要去那儿。我要买这个和那个。我觉得这个很便宜，而且很好看！那个很有意思！

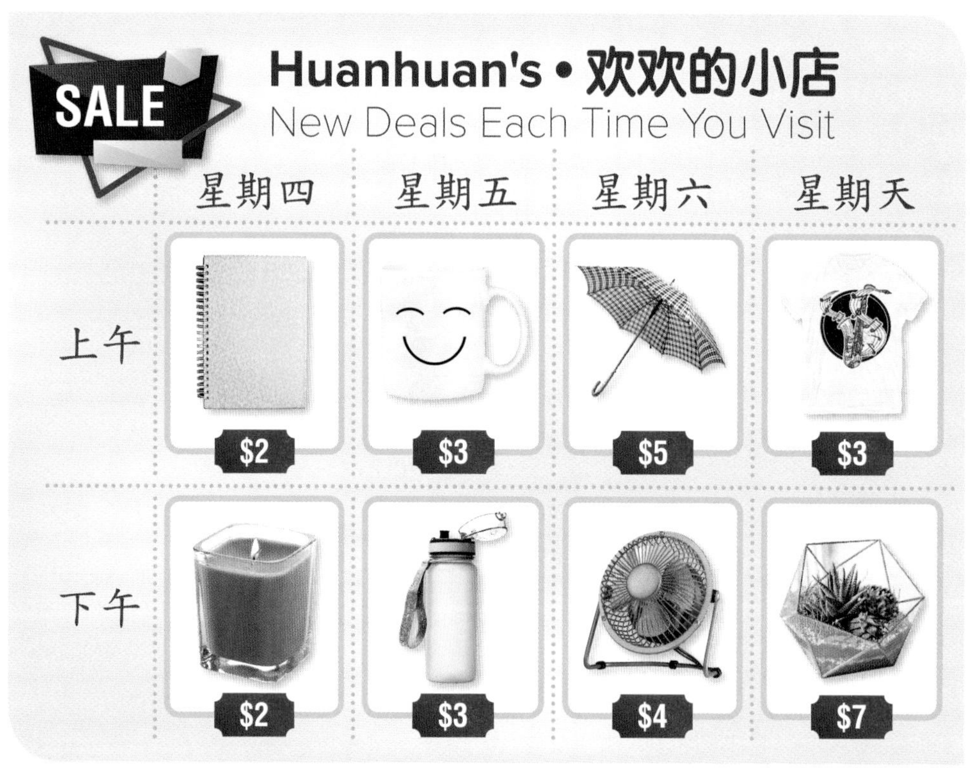

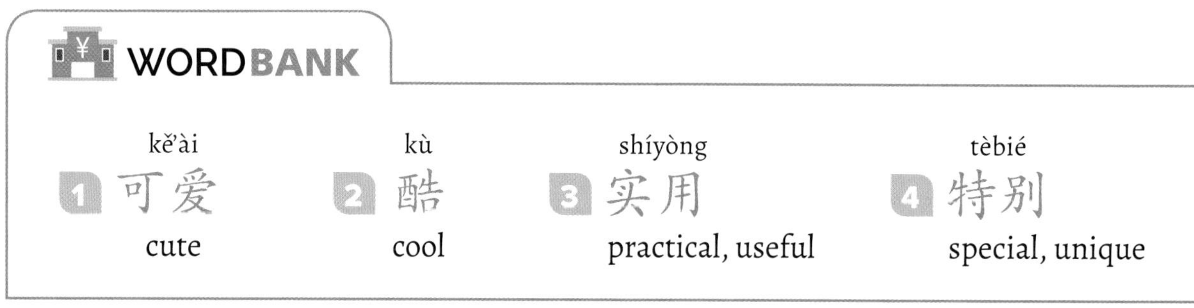

C Final Project PRESENTATIONAL

The Activities Committee

Imagine that you and your classmates are on the Activities Committee at your school. You will create a survey to find out which activity your classmates would like to add to the after-school program.

Step 1: In groups, discuss which activities you think are interesting. Refer to the Word Bank or come up with your own ideas. As a group, decide on four activities that you all find interesting.

Step 2: Write a survey to find out which of the four activities is most popular in your class. Follow the format in the example.

Example: 踢足球很有意思。　　同意 / 不同意

Step 3: Use the survey you created to learn about your classmates' opinions.

Step 4: Create a chart to show how many classmates agree or disagree with the statements in your survey. Report back to the class on how many students are interested in each activity and share the final selection with them.

WORDBANK
yóuyǒng
1 游泳
swimming
xià qí
2 下棋
playing chess
huà huà
3 画画
painting
liàn tǐcāo
4 练体操
doing gymnastics
wán fēipán
5 玩飞盘
playing frisbee
tiào wǔ
6 跳舞
dancing

Can-Do Goals

Talk with your teacher if you have questions or if you are not certain you can do the following tasks:

- Understand when others describe what they are going to do
- Talk about when you are busy and when you plan to do certain activities
- Use appropriate greetings for phone conversations
- Agree or disagree with someone
- Discuss purchasing a gift for someone
- Give simple descriptions of books and clothes

Cultural Knowledge

What did you learn about Chinese gift-giving customs?

A Birthday Dinner

CHAPTER 9

第 dì 九 jiǔ 课 kè

Martin: Mom's birthday is today! We have our gifts wrapped. Is there anything else we should do?

Isabella: I was thinking we could get some food for a nice birthday dinner. What do you think?

Martin: That sounds good! And maybe I'll play something on the erhu for Mom.

Isabella: Great! Now we just need to decide on what food to order...

Can-Do Goals

In this chapter, you will learn to:

- Talk about things you do for others
- Name some Chinese dishes and say what foods you like
- Recognize some Chinese holiday foods
- Order food from a restaurant
- Discuss completed actions
- State opinions and give reasons

CULTURE CONNECTION

měishí

Special Dishes

The Chinese proverb 民以食为天 (mín yǐ shí wéi tiān) means, roughly, "to the people, food is the most important thing," so it should come as no surprise that the preparation of special foods is central to many Chinese celebrations.

Fusion Food

In many parts of China, long life noodles, 长寿面 (chángshòumiàn), are served at birthday dinners because the long noodles carry a wish for a long life. Many Chinese people now have a cake as a part of their birthday celebrations, as well. As a result, some bakeries make fusion cakes, like this one, in the shape of a bowl of noodles.

Saying "Happy New Year" with Food

Many traditional Spring Festival foods carry positive symbolic messages. Dumplings, 饺子 (jiǎozi), symbolize wealth because their shape is similar to the ingots once used as currency in China. The word for fish, 鱼 (yú), sounds similar to the Chinese word for abundance, so fish dishes are also served at the holiday dinner.

Local Choices for Spring Festival

An elaborate feast on Spring Festival Eve is a tradition shared across China, but the menu for this meal varies depending on regional tastes and traditions. This map shows which foods are especially popular for Spring Festival dinner in different locations.

REFLECT ON THE ESSENTIAL QUESTION

How do you prepare for a special day?

1. Are there any foods that are an important part of holiday celebrations for your family?
2. Does it take a long time to prepare these foods, or do you buy them pre-made?
3. Do any of these foods have a special meaning or symbolism?

Doing things for others

1a Language Model TARGET LANGUAGE INPUT

Your teacher will lead a discussion about the images below. Try to participate as much as you can. If there is anything you don't understand, let your teacher know.

Wǒ	gěi	wǒ	jiějie	diǎn	cài.
我	给	我	姐姐	点	菜。

I am ordering food for my older sister.

Tā	gěi	tóngxúe	dǎ	diànhuà.
她	给	同学	打	电话。

She is calling her classmate.

Tā	gěi	péngyou	yì	běn	shū.
她	给	朋友	一	本	书。

She gives her friend a book.

1b New Words in Conversation INTERPRETIVE

Audio

Listen to the audio and try to understand as much as you can of Ellen and Miko's conversation as they look at a menu in a restaurant. Then read the dialogue, using the pinyin text and vocabulary list to figure out unfamiliar words.

我想吃好吃的菜，可是我不知道这种菜好吃不好吃。我不太会点菜。

Wǒ xiǎng **chī hǎochī** de **cài**, kěshì wǒ bù zhīdào zhè **zhǒng cài hǎochī** bù **hǎochī.** Wǒ bú tài huì **diǎn cài**.

我也不太会点菜。
Owen 很会点菜。
我们给他打电话吧！

Wǒ yě bú tài huì **diǎn cài**.
Owen hěn huì **diǎn cài**.
Wǒmen **gěi** tā **dǎ diànhuà** ba!

好主意！

Hǎo zhǔyi!

Comprehension Check

		T	F
1	Ellen knows what she wants to order.	○	○
2	Miko is good at ordering food.	○	○

Vocabulary

Audio

	Word	Pinyin	Meaning
1	吃	chī	to eat
2	好吃	hǎochī	tasty, delicious
3	菜	cài	a dish (of food); cuisine; vegetables
4	种	zhǒng	(measure word for kinds, sorts, types)
5	点	diǎn	to order (food)
6	给	gěi	to give; for, to
7	打电话	dǎ diànhuà	to make a phone call
8	做菜	zuòcài	to make a dish (of food)

1c Puzzle It Out PROGRESS CHECK

Complete the exercises below to check your understanding of what you learned in Section 1. If you have questions, consult the Language Reference section.

Exercise 1 Use the words in the list to complete the translation of each sentence below. Use each word only once.

好听
好看
好学

1 这种音乐很 ______。
This kind of music sounds nice.

2 我觉得这个颜色不太 ______。
I think this color is not that nice-looking.

3 我觉得中文很 ______。
I think Chinese is very easy to learn.

Exercise 2 For each sentence, choose the correct location (1 or 2) in which to add the word 给.

1 我 ___ (1) 我朋友 ___ (2) 打电话。

2 你 ___ (1) 可以 ___ (2) 我做菜吗?

3 我 ___ (1) 妈妈点 ___ (2) 好吃的菜。

5Cs
CULTURES
COMMUNITIES
COMMUNICATION
CONNECTIONS
COMPARISONS

When eating at a restaurant in China, it is common for one person to order dishes for the entire table to share. You can compliment someone who is good at ordering food by saying 你很会点菜! This means that he or she understands which dishes everyone will find tasty, is good at ordering dishes that work well for the occasion, and remembers to order a variety of different types of food. Do you share food when you go out to eat with friends and family?

Language Reference

1 好 + verb

In some cases, a positive adjective (description word) is created when certain verbs are added to 好. Here are some common examples:

Structure	Meaning	Example
好 + 看 good + see, look at	good-looking, nice-looking, enjoyable to watch (for movies), enjoyable to read (for books)	你觉得这个颜色好看吗? Do you think this is a nice color? 这个电影很好看! This movie is really good!
好 + 吃 (chī) good + eat	tasty, delicious	这个菜(cài)很好吃(hǎochī)! This dish is delicious!
好 + 听 good + hear, listen to	pleasant to hear	我觉得这种(zhǒng)音乐很好听。 I think this kind of music is really nice.

In other cases, 好 + verb can be translated to "easy to do" in English, as in these examples:

Structure	Meaning	Example
好 + 学 good + study, learn	easy to learn	中文很好学! Chinese is easy to learn!
好 + 做 good + make, do	easy to make or do	中国菜(cài)好做吗? Is Chinese food easy to make?

2 The many uses of 给

Often, the word 给 (gěi) simply means "to give."

			gěi						
1	你	可以	给	我	那	本	书	吗?	= Can you give me that book?
	You	can	give	me	that		book	?	

At other times, the meaning of 给 (gěi) can be translated as "to" or "for," and 给 (gěi) is followed by the person (or thing) receiving the action. For example:

		gěi		diǎn cài	
2	我	给	你	点菜。	= I'll order food for you.
	I	for	you	order food	

			gěi				cài	
3	他	可以	给	你	做	这个	菜。	= He can make this dish for you.
	He	can	for	you	make	this	dish	

		gěi		dǎ diànhuà		
4	我	给	爸爸	打电话	吧。	= Let me give Dad a call.
	I	to	father	make a phone call		

1d Using the Language INTERPERSONAL

Activity 1 Your e-pal from China wants to do something nice for his family, and he's asked you to help him come up with ideas. Working with a partner, jot down ideas of things that he could do for his 奶奶 (nǎinai) (grandmother on father's side), 妈妈, and 弟弟. Use the Word Bank to help you.

Examples:

他可以给奶奶 (nǎinai) 打电话。

他可以给妈妈弹吉他。

WORDBANK
1
zuò jiāwù
做家务
do chores
2
mǎi cài
买菜
buy groceries
3
dú shū
读书
read (to someone else)

Activity 2 What kind of music is 很好听? What sort of food is 好吃? Find out what your classmates think.

Step 1: Rate each item in the chart that follows. Use a scale of 很好, 好, 不太好, or 不好.

Step 2: Ask the other students in your group about their preferences. Use the example sentences below to start the conversation. Take notes about the preferences of your groupmates.

Step 3: Share your group's preferences with the rest of the class.

Example sentences:

你觉得这种音乐好听吗？ 你觉得这种电影好看吗？

你觉得这种乐器好学吗？ 你觉得这个菜好吃吗？

	A	B	C	D
音乐				
电影				
乐器	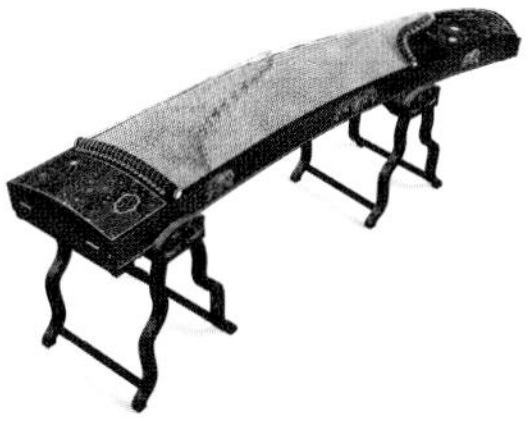			
菜				

Talking about yesterday

2a Language Model TARGET LANGUAGE INPUT

Your teacher will lead a discussion about the images below. Try to participate as much as you can. If there is anything you don't understand, let your teacher know.

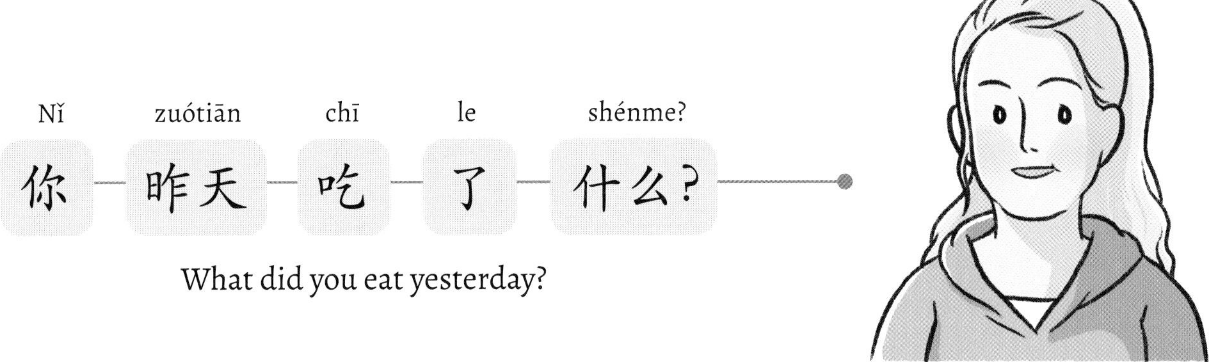

Nǐ zuótiān chī le shénme?
你 昨天 吃 了 什么?
What did you eat yesterday?

2b New Words in Conversation INTERPRETIVE

Listen to the audio and try to understand as much as you can. Then read the dialogue, using the pinyin text and vocabulary list to figure out unfamiliar words.

我们今天吃饺子吧！ Wǒmen jīntiān chī jiǎozi ba!

今天我不想吃饺子。 Jīntiān wǒ bù xiǎng chī jiǎozi.
我昨天吃了饺子。你呢？ Wǒ zuótiān chī le jiǎozi. Nǐ ne?
你昨天吃了什么？ Nǐ zuótiān chī le shénme?

我昨天去了饭馆。 Wǒ zuótiān qù le fànguǎn.
我吃了一份面条和 Wǒ chī le yí fèn miàntiáo hé
两份红烧肉。 liǎng fèn hóngshāo ròu.

你喜欢吃肉吗？ Nǐ xǐhuan chī ròu ma?

对啊！肉很好吃！ Duì a! Ròu hěn hǎochī!

Comprehension Check

		T	F
1	Owen wants to have dumplings today.	○	○
2	Ellen agrees to eat dumplings. 	○	○
3	Owen went to a restaurant yesterday.	○	○
4	Owen had one serving of noodles and three servings of red-cooked pork.	○	○
5	Owen doesn't like meat very much.	○	○

Audio

Vocabulary

	Word	Pinyin	Meaning
9	饺子	jiǎozi	dumplings (with vegetable and/or meat filling)
10	昨天	zuótiān	yesterday
11	了	le	(a word that indicates an action is complete)
12	饭馆	fànguǎn	restaurant
13	份	fèn	(measure word for a portion/serving of something)
14	面条	miàntiáo	noodles
15	红烧	hóngshāo	to braise in soy sauce (to red-cook)
16	肉	ròu	meat (frequently pork)

2c Puzzle It Out PROGRESS CHECK

Complete the exercise below to check your understanding of what you learned in Section 2. If you have questions, consult the Language Reference section.

Complete the sentences below by adding 吧 , 吗 , or 了 .

1 我们明天去看电影 ____！

2 我昨天去饭馆 ____。

3 你今天有空 ____？

4 你昨天吃 ____ 面条 ____？

5 我们点一份面条 ____。

3 Using 了 to talk about completed actions

了 (le) is a word with a lot of uses, and one of the most common is to indicate that an action has been completed. 了 (le) can appear after a verb or at the end of a sentence.

zuótiān le
1 他昨天看电影了。 He saw a movie yesterday.

zuótiān le
2 你昨天吃了什么？ What did you eat yesterday?

le miàntiáo
3 我吃了面条。 I ate noodles.

TAKE NOTE

Usually, when 了 (le) is used the action is complete and happened in the past. However, the completed action can sometimes be in the future!

le
明天她和同学买了衣服去看电影。

Tomorrow, she and her classmates will go to the movies after shopping for clothes.

If the action did not take place or was not completed, put 没有 or just 没 in front of the verb. (不 is not used in this case.)

zuótiān fànguǎn le
A: 你们昨天去饭馆了吗？ Did you go to a restaurant yesterday?

zuótiān fànguǎn
B: 我昨天没有去饭馆。 I did not go to a restaurant yesterday.

C: 我也没去。 I didn't either.

To answer 了 (le) questions more briefly, simply repeat the verb with 了 (le) or say 没有.

A:	你们昨天(zuótiān)去了(le)饭馆(fànguǎn)吗?	Did you go to a restaurant yesterday?
B:	去了(le)。	(Yes,) I went (to a restaurant).
C:	没有。	(No,) I didn't.

2d Using the Language INTERPERSONAL

Create one card for each of the activities listed below. On each card you will write a sentence saying either that you did or did not do that activity yesterday. Then play a collecting game with your classmates! Go around the room and ask your classmates if they did the activity on one of your cards. If your classmate's answer is the same as yours, take the card! Then your classmate will have a turn to ask you a question. See how many cards you can collect.

Activities:

吃面条，吃饺子，吃红烧肉，去饭馆，踢足球，打篮球，打电话，看电影，学中文

What a Character!

shí 饣 — 1 — 2 — 3

This component is derived from the character 食 (shí), which means "food." The component 饣 is usually found on the left side of characters.

Can you identify the character component 饣 (shí) in the words below?

1 饺子

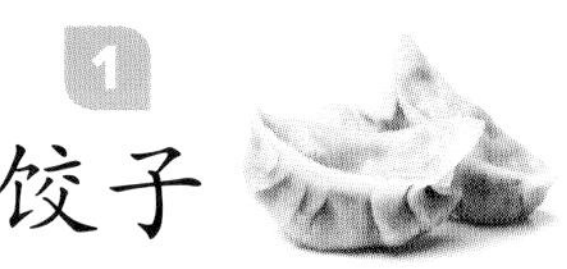

2 馄饨

3 月饼

4 米饭

Asking and answering the question "why?"

3a Language Model

TARGET LANGUAGE INPUT

Your teacher will lead a discussion about the image below. Try to participate as much as you can. If there is anything you don't understand, let your teacher know.

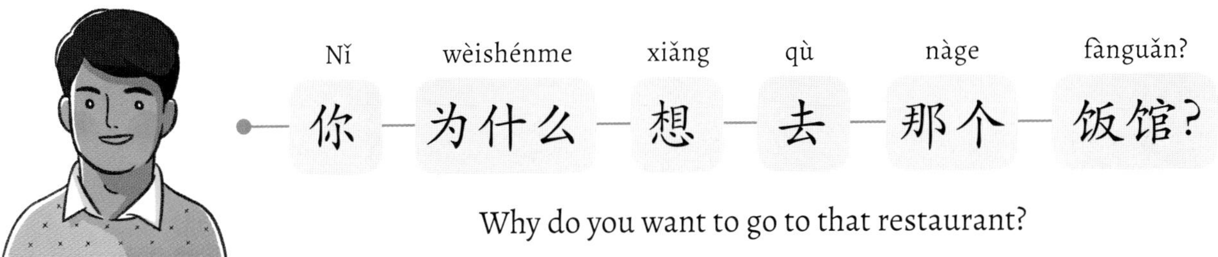

Nǐ wèishénme xiǎng qù nàge fànguǎn?
你为什么想去那个饭馆？

Why do you want to go to that restaurant?

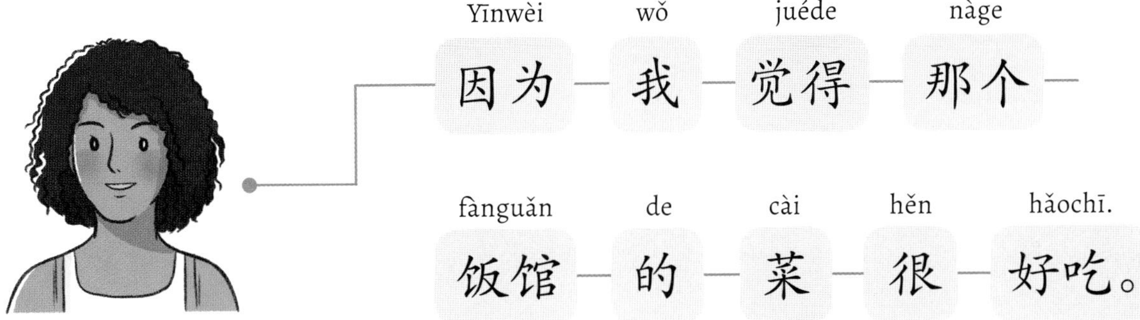

Yīnwèi wǒ juéde nàge fànguǎn de cài hěn hǎochī.
因为我觉得那个饭馆的菜很好吃。

Because I think that restaurant's food is tasty.

Audio

3b New Words in Conversation INTERPRETIVE

Listen to the audio and try to understand as much as you can. Then read the dialogue, using the pinyin text and vocabulary list to figure out unfamiliar words.

祝你生日快乐！今天我们去那个美国饭馆吧！ — Zhù nǐ shēngrì kuàilè! Jīntiān wǒmen qù nàge Měiguó fànguǎn ba!

我不想去那个饭馆。 — Wǒ bù xiǎng qù nàge fànguǎn.

你为什么不想去？ — Nǐ wèishénme bù xiǎng qù?

因为我觉得那个饭馆的菜不好吃，所以我不想去。 — Yīnwèi wǒ juéde nàge fànguǎn de cài bù hǎochī, suǒyǐ wǒ bù xiǎng qù.

那我们去中国饭馆吧！那儿有很多好吃的菜。 — Nà wǒmen qù Zhōngguó fàngguǎn ba! Nàr yǒu hěn duō hǎochī de cài.

Comprehension Check

		T	F
1	Today is Sanjay's birthday.	○	○
2	Sanjay suggests they go to a Chinese restaurant.	○	○

Audio

Vocabulary

	Word	Pinyin	Meaning
17	祝	zhù	to wish (well)
18	快乐	kuàilè	happy
19	为什么	wèishénme	why
20	因为	yīnwèi	because
21	所以	suǒyǐ	so, therefore
22	多	duō	many, much, lots

3c Puzzle It Out PROGRESS CHECK

Complete the exercise below to check your understanding of what you learned in Section 3. If you have questions, consult the Language Reference section.

Create logical sentences by connecting each 因为 phrase in the left column to a 所以 phrase in the right column.

1	因为那个饭馆有很多人，	a	所以我很会弹古筝。
2	因为今天是我的生日，	b	所以我想吃面条。
3	因为我经常弹，	c	所以我不想去那个饭馆。

Language Reference

4 Giving a reason

In Chinese, speakers may use 因为 to express a cause or reason, and 所以 to express a result. However, unlike English, these two words can be used in the same sentence to emphasize a cause-and-effect relationship.

1 我点了两份红烧肉，因为(yīnwèi)我觉得红烧肉很好吃。

I ordered two servings of red-cooked pork because I think red-cooked pork is delicious.

2 中国菜很好吃，所以(suǒyǐ)我经常去中国饭馆。

Chinese food is delicious, so I often go to Chinese restaurants.

3 因为(yīnwèi)我觉得古筝很好听，所以(suǒyǐ)我很想学。

I think the guzheng sounds nice, so I really want to learn to play it. (Or: Because I think the guzheng sounds nice, I really want to learn to play it.)

3d Using the Language INTERPERSONAL

For this task, you will compare your opinions with those of your classmates.

Step 1: Look at the pairs of items below and think about which item you prefer and why. Refer to the list of possible reasons to help explain why you prefer the item you chose.

Step 2: Once the class is broken into groups, talk to your groupmates and ask them for their opinions. Keep track of their responses to discuss with the class. Reminder: Use 这个 when pointing to the image in each pair that is closer to you and 那个 when pointing to the image that is farther away from you.

Step 3: Share your group's preferences with the rest of the class.

Example:

Student A: 你喜欢这个还是那个?

Student B: 因为我觉得这个很难，所以我喜欢那个。

Possible Reasons:

(不)好看，(不)好听，(不)好学，(不)好吃，
(不)好做，(没)有意思，贵，便宜，简单，难

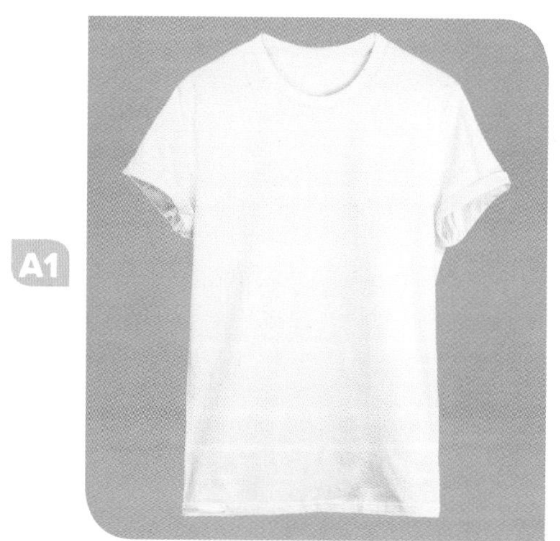

B1

B2

C1

C2

LANGUAGE
CHALLENGE

For birthdays, Chinese people sing the familiar tune "Happy Birthday to You." Chinese people don't say the person's name when they are singing the song though. Try singing the birthday song in Chinese!

祝 你 生 日 快 乐 祝 你 生 日 快
乐 祝 你 生 日 快 乐 祝 你 生 日 快
乐

Put the Pieces Together!

Audio

A Reading and Listening INTERPRETIVE

Passage 1

MARTIN AND ISABELLA ARE TRYING TO FIGURE OUT WHAT TO ORDER FOR THEIR MOM'S BIRTHDAY DINNER.

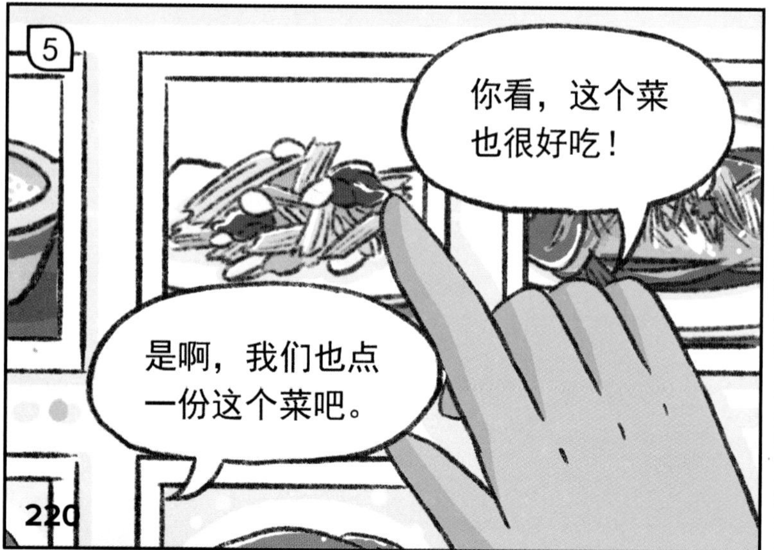

7
我们给这个饭馆
打电话吧？
好啊！

8
喂，你好！
你好！
今天是我妈妈的生日，
我想点菜。

9
我想点……
……

10
好，一份饺子、
一份红烧肉、
一份面条、一份……
面条？
可是我们没有点面条……

11
因为今天是
你妈妈的生日，
所以我们送她
一份面条！
谢谢！

12

祝你生日快乐，祝你生日快乐……

谢谢你们！二胡很好听！

Comprehension Check 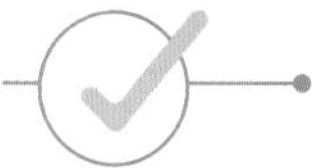

		T	F
1	Martin wants to eat dumplings.	○	○
2	Isabella calls the restaurant to order noodles.	○	○
3	The waiter gives Isabella a free serving of noodles because she ordered so much food.	○	○
4	Martin plays the erhu for his mom.	○	○

Passage 2 Read the Chinese menu and count how many dishes feature noodles, how many dishes feature meat, and how many dishes feature vegetables. Bonus: Are there any other characters you recognize?

饿龙饭馆			
回锅肉	3.00	担担面	11.00
炒面	8.00	鱼香肉丝	10.00
炒饭	6.00	蒜炒菠菜	5.00
牛肉面	9.00	蔬菜水饺	7.00

Passage 3 Listen to the conversation. Are the following statements true (T) or false (F)?

Audio

		T	F
1	The girl wants to eat red-cooked pork today.	○	○
2	The boy's mom made red-cooked pork yesterday.	○	○
3	The boy thinks dumplings are really tasty.	○	○

Passage 4 Owen and his family went out to eat. Listen to the description of each person's food preferences. Which dish do you think Owen ordered for each person?

Audio

A 

B 

C 

D 

1 Owen's mom

2 Owen's younger brother

3 Owen's older sister

4 Owen

B Speaking INTERPERSONAL

Your school is throwing the Chinese exchange students a send-off party, and your Chinese class has been asked to help plan it! To help you, the exchange students' classmates have provided some information about what the Chinese students like. In groups, discuss the profile of one of the exchange students. Decide on one thing you could give to the student, and one thing you could do for him or her. Be ready to share your suggestions with the class!

Example:

A: 因为天天喜欢吃面条，所以我们想给她点一份面条。

B: 好主意。你们想送她什么？

A: 因为她喜欢学英文，所以我们想送她一本英文书。

天天

Likes studying English

Likes noodles of all kinds

Loves animals

明明

Likes playing basketball

Likes watching sci-fi movies

Loves meat

春春

Likes music

Likes reading

Loves blue

京京

Likes comics

Likes green

Is vegetarian

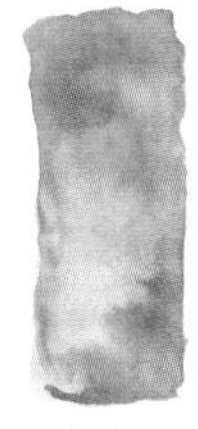

1 lánsè 蓝色 blue

2 lǜsè 绿色 green

3 mànhuà shū 漫画书 comic book(s)

4 kēhuàn diànyǐng 科幻电影 sci-fi movie(s)

C Final Project PRESENTATIONAL

Chinese Diary

You will write a diary entry describing the events of three days — yesterday, today, and tomorrow. You may write about yourself or about a character you imagine.

Step 1: Brainstorm the activities and events you want to write about.

Step 2: Write a diary entry describing yesterday, today, and tomorrow. Make sure to talk about what you (or your character) liked or didn't like about what happened.

Step 3: Practice reading the diary entry aloud. Your teacher may have you read to the class or record yourself reading.

Can-Do Goals

Talk with your teacher if you have questions or if you are not certain you can do the following tasks:

- Talk about things you do for others
- Name some Chinese dishes and say what foods you like
- Recognize some Chinese holiday foods
- Order food from a restaurant
- Discuss completed actions
- State opinions and give reasons

Cultural Knowledge

What did you learn about Chinese celebratory foods?

Making dumplings for the Spring Festival celebration

Photo Credits

Every effort has been made to accurately credit the copyright owners of materials reproduced in this publication. Omissions brought to our attention will be corrected in subsequent editions.

Unit 1 Opener

p.1, Art_Photo/Shutterstock.com; **p.2,** Monkey Business Images/Shutterstock.com

Chapter 1

p.8, Data courtesy of Marc Imhoff/NASA GSFC and Christopher Elvidge/NOAA NGDC, Image by Craig Mayhew and Robert Simmon/NASA GSFC; Shan_shan/Shutterstock.com; **p.9,** PKartstudio/Shutterstock.com; popular.vector/Shutterstock.com; Illizium/Shutterstock.com; Fenton one/Shutterstock.com; rickyd/Shutterstock.com; **p.10,** Sean Pavone/Shutterstock.com; Sven Hansche/Shutterstock.com; HelloRF Zcool/Shutterstock.com; **p.11,** eenevski/Shutterstock.com; **p.16,** exopixel/Shutterstock.com; **p.19,** hfzimages/Shutterstock.com; **p.20,** Patrick Lin/Shutterstock.com; **p.23,** mark stephens photography/Shutterstock.com; Victor Wong/Shutterstock.com; Uwe Aranas/Shutterstock.com; Watch The World/Shutterstock.com; **p.24,** Chris Howey/Shutterstock.com; antoniodiaz/Shutterstock.com; Rawpixel.com/Shutterstock.com; **p.26,** hfzimages/Shutterstock.com

Chapter 2

p.30, photos for composite image by michaeljung/Shutterstock.com; **p.34,** Georgios Kollidas/Shutterstock.com; Marion S. Trikosko; catwalker/Shutterstock.com; DFree/Shutterstock.com; **p.35,** Atstock Productions/Shutterstock.com; Dean Drobot/Shutterstock.com; **p.39,** photos for composite image by Silatip/Shutterstock.com, Vitalli Petrushenko/Shutterstock.com, Mega Pixel/Shutterstock.com, and OlekStock/Shutterstock.com; **p.40,** wavebreakmedia/Shutterstock.com; Monkey Business Images/Shutterstock.com; Dean Drobot/Shutterstock.com; **p.48,** photos for composite images by lalan/Shutterstock.com; **p.49,** michaeljung/Shutterstock.com; Rawpixel.com/Shutterstock.com; Monkey Business Images/Shutterstock.com; Kzenon/Shutterstock.com; **p.50,** Akugasahagy/Shutterstock.com; tratong/Shutterstock.com; Mega Pixel/Shutterstock.com; Africa Studio/Shutterstock.com; Kozak Sergii/Shutterstock.com; **p.52,** Atstock Productions/Shutterstock.com

Chapter 3

p.54, Monkey Business Images/Shutterstock.com; A. Aleksandravicius/Shutterstock.com; **p. 56,** Animashka/Shutterstock.com; **p.60,** Syda Productions/Shutterstock.com; silverkblackstock/Shutterstock.com; **p.61,** michaeljung/Shutterstock.com; iko/Shutterstock.com; **p.65,** iStock.com/NicolasMcComber; **p.68,** Napat/Shutterstock.com; Zharinova Marina/Shutterstock.com; **p.73,** Daria Medvedeva/Shutterstock.com; **p.74,** iStock.com/DGLimages; **p.76,** iStock.com/yanjf

Unit 2 Opener

p.77, Maridav/Shutterstock.com; **p.78,** Yuganov Konstantin/Shutterstock.com

Chapter 4

p.80, Alex V-N/Shutterstock.com; Hung Chung Chih/Shutterstock.com; **p.81,** iStock.com/fototrav; **p.82,** Juriah Mosin/Shutterstock.com; **p.86,** ekler/Shutterstock.com; **p.87,** Monkey Business Images/Shutterstock.com; Mike_shots/Shutterstock.com; **p.92,** LP2 Studio/Shutterstock.com; Shanti Hesse/Shutterstock.com; YANG YIDONG/Shutterstock.com; Paul_Brighton/Shutterstock.com; Hung Chung Chih/Shutterstock.com; Hung Chung Chih/Shutterstock.com; **p.93,** Monkey Business Images/Shutterstock.com; Monkey Business Images/Shutterstock.com; **p.97,** tanpanamanoob/Shutterstock.com; **p.98,** DW labs Incorporated/Shutterstock.com; **p.104,** testing/Shutterstock.com

Chapter 5

p.106, axz700/Shutterstock.com; chinahbzyg/Shutterstock.com; **p.108,** doomu/Shutterstock.com; Chones/Shutterstock.com; pukach/Shutterstock.com; irin-k/Shutterstock.com; **p.111,** Yosuke Hasegawa/Shutterstock.com; **p.112,** imtmphoto/Shutterstock.com; **p.116,** StockSmartStart/Shutterstock.com; **p.117,** Uwe Aranas/Shutterstock.com; **p.120,** Fotokon/Shutterstock.com; **p.121,** Ronald Sumners/Shutterstock.com; Jaren Jai Wicklund/Shutterstock.com; SeventyFour/Shutterstock.com; fizkes/Shutterstock.com; Pixel-Shot/Shutterstock.com; Merla/Shutterstock.com; **p.125,** Yingchun Guan/Cheng & Tsui; **p.127,** Dark ink/Shutterstock.com; ProStockStudio/Shutterstock.com; Mary Long/Shutterstock.com; sayu/Shutterstock.com; **p.128,** xian-photos/Shutterstock.com

Chapter 6

p.130, aphotostory/Shutterstock.com; **p.131,** Marian Stacey/Cheng & Tsui; **p.132,** 21 Phukao/Shutterstock.com; Shan_shan/Shutterstock.com; jianqing diao/Shutterstock.com; del Monaco/Shutterstock.com; **p.135,** sleepingpanda/Shutterstock.com; **p.136,** Iakov Filimonov/Shutterstock.com; **p.139,** photos for composite image by Mau Horng/Shutterstock.com, Ryzhkov Oleksandr/Shutterstock.com, Topconcept/Shutterstock.com, Boris Medvedev/Shutterstock.com, DucMityagov/Shutterstock.com, sumire8/Shutterstock.com, ILYA AKINSHIN/Shutterstock.com, and zydesign/Shutterstock.com; **p.140,** Asia Images Group/

Shutterstock.com; **p.148,** photos for composite image by sumire8/Shutterstock.com and Boris Medvedev/Shutterstock.com; **p.150,** Thammanoon Panyakham/Shutterstock.com

Unit 3 Opener

p.151, Sergei Bachlakov/Shutterstock.com; **p.152,** Elena Nichizhenova/Shutterstock.com

Chapter 7

p.154, Mcimage/Shutterstock.com; magentayi/Shutterstock.com; **p.155,** CookieWei/Shutterstock.com; **p.156,** inewsfoto/Shutterstock.com; **p.160,** Freer/Shutterstock.com; **p.161,** photos for composite image by zydesign/Shutterstock.com, STUDIO DREAM/Shutterstock.com, chyworks/Shutterstock.com, and notkoo/Shutterstock.com; **p.166,** photos for composite image by deedl/Shutterstock.com, Hobort/Shutterstock.com, vertolena/Shutterstock.com, mahey/Shutterstock.com, Satika/Shutterstock.com, Skorik Ekaterina/Shutterstock.com, Le Panda/Shutterstock.com, cobalt88/Shutterstock.com, AmazeinDesign/Shutterstock.com, CKA/Shutterstock.com, Maxito/Shutterstock.com, Vector Tradition/Shutterstock.com, and Khartseva Tetiana/Shutterstock.com; **p.167,** pogonici/Shutterstock.com; **p.170,** photos for composite image by Who is Danny/Shutterstock.com, favorita1987/Shutterstock.com, Tapui/Shutterstock.com, Thomas Pajot/Shutterstock.com, Meth Mehr/Shutterstock.com, MicrostockStudio/Shutterstock.com, New Africa/Shutterstock.com, studiovin/Shutterstock.com, Africa Studio/Shutterstock.com, paseven/Shutterstock.com, and Astrovector/Shutterstock.com; **p.174,** Pirina/Shutterstock.com; November27/Shutterstock.com; enchanted_fairy/Shutterstock.com; animicsgo/Shutterstock.com; **p.175,** Studio Peace/Shutterstock.com; Radu Razvan/Shutterstock.com; LightField Studios/Shutterstock.com; Iakov Filimonov/Shutterstock.com; **p.176,** iStock.com/beijingstory

Chapter 8

p.178, The_Molostock/Shutterstock.com; gracethang2/Shutterstock.com; **p.179,** GOLFX/Shutterstock.com; Freer/Shutterstock.com; **p.180,** LightField Studios/Shutterstock.com; zhu difeng/Shutterstock.com; LightField Studios/Shutterstock.com; Fotokostic/Shutterstock.com; LightField Studios/Shutterstock.com; **p.185,** Africa Studio/Shutterstock.com; Africa Studio/Shutterstock.com; Tim Large/Shutterstock.com; alexlibris/Shutterstock.com; **p.188,** feelplus/Shutterstock.com; Dima Moroz/Shutterstock.com; Piraha Photos/Shutterstock.com; horiyan/Shutterstock.com; **p.189,** photos for composite image by OZaiachin/Shutterstock.com, Magdalena Wielobob/Shutterstock.com, Hekla/Shutterstock.com, and gogoiso/Shutterstock.com; **p.192,** imagewriter/Shutterstock.com; **p.193,** humphery/Shutterstock.com; jianbing Lee/Shutterstock.com; Yuangeng Zhang/Shutterstock.com; iStock.com/tanukiphoto; **p.197,** photos for composite image by piotr_pabijan/Shutterstock.com, Natali Glado/Shutterstock.com, Prokrida/Shutterstock.com, sahua d/Shutterstock.com, robuart/Shutterstock.com, and krkt/Shutterstock.com; **p.198,** Oleg Golovnev/Shutterstock.com; paikong/Shutterstock.com; Den Rozhnovsky/Shutterstock.com; intueri/Shutterstock.com; James Hoenstine/Shutterstock.com; Kartinkin77/Shutterstock.com; PROFFIPhoto/Shutterstock.com; Dzina Belskaya/Shutterstock.com; **p.199,** MF production/Shutterstock.com; Robert Adrian Hillman/Shutterstock.com; Eroshka/Shutterstock.com; sportpoint/Shutterstock.com; Kluva/Shutterstock.com; Passiflora/Shutterstock.com; Christos Georghiou/Shutterstock.com; **p.200,** paulaphoto/Shutterstock.com

Chapter 9

p.202, Muhamad_Firdaus/Shutterstock.com; yuda chen/Shutterstock.com; **p.203,** photos for composite image by Peter Hermes Furian/Shutterstock.com, HelloRF Zcool/Shutterstock.com, bonchan/Shutterstock.com, and Shah Affendy/Shutterstock.com; **p.204,** Denys Prykhodov/Shutterstock.com; arek_malang/Shutterstock.com; LightField Studios; **p.206,** silver.B/Shutterstock.com; **p.208,** DeymosHR/Shutterstock.com; Syda Productions/Shutterstock.com; Oksana Kuzmina/Shutterstock.com; **p.209,** Jason Stitt/Shutterstock.com; LightField Studios/Shutterstock.com; Stokkete/Shutterstock.com; Dmitry Lobanov/Shutterstock.com; Everett Collection/Shutterstock.com; TuiPhotoEngineer/Shutterstock.com; Gorodenkoff/Shutterstock.com; vectorpouch/Shutterstock.com; Topconcept/Shutterstock.com; Svilen G/Shutterstock.com; Kayo/Shutterstock.com; Chinaview/Shutterstock.com; Digital Painting/Shutterstock.com; Cyril Hou/Shutterstock.com; Ekaterina Kondratova/Shutterstock.com; Elena Shashkina/Shutterstock.com; **p.210,** yuda chen/Shutterstock.com; HelloRF Zcool/Shutterstock.com; HelloRF Zcool/Shutterstock.com; **p.214,** JIANG HONGYAN/Shutterstock.com; Tommy Studio/Shutterstock.com; Topphy/Shutterstock.com; SOMMAI/Shutterstock.com; **p.215,** Monkey Business Images/Shutterstock.com; **p.218,** Dmitry Zimin/Shutterstock.com; elenovsky/Shutterstock.com; **p.219,** Dani Vincek/Shutterstock.com; Eugenia Lucasenco/Shutterstock.com; WLTeoh/Shutterstock.com; Vigen M/Shutterstock.com; **p.223,** L.F./Shutterstock.com; bonchan/Shutterstock.com; HelloRF Zcool/Shutterstock.com; OlesyaSH/Shutterstock.com; **p.224,** atiger/Shutterstock.com; Tom Wang/Shutterstock.com; rongyiquan/Shutterstock.com; Tom Wang/Shutterstock.com; Yaangiji/Shutterstock.com; Yaangiji/Shutterstock.com; benchart/Shutterstock.com; photos for composite image by VTT Studio/Shutterstock.com and Tithi Luadthong/Shutterstock.com; **p.225,** Monkey Business Images/Shutterstock.com; **p.226,** XiXinXing/Shutterstock.com

Appendix: Guide to Pronunciation

Initials

Below is a table listing all the initials in Mandarin. Listen to the audio to learn how each initial is pronounced as part of a Mandarin syllable.

In the audio, each initial is first said together with a simple final, either u or ü. This will allow you to focus on the pronunciation of the initials. You will then hear an example word using the initial. The list below shows each example word written in pinyin and then in Chinese characters, followed by the Chapter and Section in which the example word is introduced in the textbook.

	Sound	Example Word
1	b	bā (八 : 1.5)
2	c	cài (菜 : 9.1)
3	ch	chǒngwù (宠物 : 3.3)
4	d	de (的 : 2.1)
5	f	fànguǎn (饭馆 : 9.2)
6	g	gēge (哥哥 : 3.1)
7	h	hǎo (好 : 1.6)
8	j	jiǔ (九 : 1.5)
9	k	kàn (看 : 3.2)
10	l	lǎoshī (老师 : 1.6)
11	m	māma (妈妈 : 3.1)
12	n	nǐ (你 : 1.6)

	Sound	Example Word
13	p	péngyou (朋友 : 2.3)
14	q	qī (七 : 1.5)
15	r	rén (人 : 4.1)
16	s	sān (三 : 1.5)
17	sh	shéi (谁 : 2.2)
18	t	tā (她 : 2.2)
19	w	wèn (问 : 7.3)
20	x	xuéshēng (学生 : 1.6)
21	y	yǒu (有 : 2.2)
22	z	zàijiàn (再见 : 1.6)
23	zh	zhī (只 : 3.3)

Special Consonants

Many letters are pronounced the same, or nearly so, in Mandarin and English. However, Mandarin also has sounds that English does not have, and the spelling of words in pinyin may not reflect the sounds you would expect.

In English, there is one j sound, one ch sound, and one sh sound. Mandarin splits each of these sounds into a pair of consonants, one with your tongue right behind your teeth, and one with your tongue further back in your mouth. Different letters are used in pinyin to represent these different sounds.

Audio

English	Pinyin Initial, Front of Mouth	Example Word	Pinyin Initial, Back of Mouth	Example Word
j	**1** j	jǐ (几：3.1)	**2** zh	zhè (这：4.2)
ch	**3** q	qī (七：1.5)	**4** ch	chǎng (场：5.2)
sh	**5** x	xué (学：4.1)	**6** sh	shéi (谁：2.2)

The sounds represented by the letters z, c, and r in pinyin are also quite different from their sounds in English.

The Mandarin initial r can be an especially difficult sound; although it is shown as an r, it is pronounced quite differently from the English r. To make this sound, try making the j sound in the French word Jacques while also adding a bit of the English r sound. This is approximately what the Mandarin r sounds like when used as an initial.

Audio

Pinyin Initial	Similar English Sound	Mandarin Example Word
1 z	"ds," as in "ads," "kids"	zài (在：4.3)
2 c	"ts," as in "cats," "nets"	cài (菜：9.1)
3 r	"j," as in "Jacques"	rén (人：4.1)

Simple Finals

There are six simple finals in Mandarin. In the audio, each simple final is first pronounced by itself, and then an example word is given. Where possible, the example words are taken from the vocabulary introduced in this textbook.

Something to note: when the simple finals i and u are used at the beginning of a syllable, they are written as y and w. So the initials y and w that were introduced previously sound exactly the same as i and u; ya = ia, wan = uan, etc.

Simple Final		Similar English Sound	Example Word
1	a	"a" in "father"	bā (八: 1.5)
2	o	"o" in "more"	mò (末: 7.2)
3	e	Part way between "e" in "bet" and "u" in "but"	gè (个: 3.1)
4	i	"ee" in "meet" *	nǐ (你: 1.6)
5	u	"oo" in "too" *	bù (不: 1.6)
6	ü	Part way between "ee" in "meet" and "oo" in "too"	qù (去: 5.2)

Audio

*There are exceptions, which will be explained in the Variable Vowels section.

Variable Vowels

For the most part, you will naturally pick up on the vowel sounds as you hear them repeated. To help you tackle some variable ones, here is a guide to a couple of Mandarin vowels that are different from English vowels.

One of the trickiest vowels for many learners is the vowel ü, which is a sound English doesn't have. Here's one way to try saying this sound: Say "ee," and, while still saying "ee," round your lips like you are trying to say "oo." You will only see this sound written with the two dots over the u when it follows an l or n. When the ü sound comes after y, j, q, or x, it is written simply as u, but beware: it is still pronounced as ü. This rule will also apply to the compound finals introduced later in the Appendix. For instance, the pinyin "xue" should be pronounced as "xüe," such as in xuéshēng (学生), and the pinyin "yun" should be pronounced as "yün," such as in yùndòng (运动).

Words with ü sound		Meaning
1	nǚ	female
2	lǜ	green
3	yú	fish
4	jǔ	to lift, to raise
5	qù	to go
6	xǔ	to permit, to promise

Audio

The vowel **i** is another occasionally tricky vowel in Mandarin. In most cases, this vowel sounds like "ee." However, the vowel **i** is not pronounced "ee" when it comes after **z**, **c**, **s**, **zh**, **ch**, **sh**, or **r**. In these cases, simply extend the sound you are already making with the consonant. For example, the Chinese word sì (四) is pronounced similar to "sss," not like "see."

Audio

Like "ee"	Not like "ee"
1 lí	2 zǐ
3 qī	4 chī
5 dì	6 sì

Compound Finals

Once you have learned the pronunciation of simple finals, compound finals should not be too difficult to pronounce. In the audio, each compound final is first pronounced by itself, and then an example word is given. Where possible, the example words are taken from the vocabulary introduced in this textbook.

Audio

Compound Final	Example Word	Compound Final	Example Word
1 ai	zài (在:4.3)	16 iang	xiǎng (想:5.2)
2 ei	mèimei (妹妹:3.1)	17 ing	tīng (听:6.3)
3 ao	hǎo (好:1.6)	18 iong	xióng (熊, bear)
4 ou	dōu (都:4.1)	19 ua	huā (花, flower)
5 an	sān (三:1.5)	20 uo	zuò (做:5.3)
6 en	hěn (很:3.2)	21 uai	kuài (快:9.3)
7 ang	chǎng (场:5.2)	22 ui (u + ei)	duì (对:4.1)
8 eng	shēng (生:1.6)	23 uan	guǎn (馆:5.3)
9 ong	sòng (送:8.3)	24 un	chūn (春:2.2)
10 ia	jiā (家:4.3)	25 uang	chuáng (床, bed)
11 iao	jiào (叫:2.1)	26 üe	xué (学:4.1)
12 ie	jiějie (姐姐:3.1)	27 üan*	xuǎn (选, to choose)
13 iu (i + ou)	liù (六:1.5)	28 ün	yùn (运:5.3)
14 ian*	diàn (店:6.2)	29 er	èr (二 :1.5)
15 in	Lín (林:2.2)		

* In these finals the -an sound is pronounced so quickly that it sounds similar to the English "en" in "when."

Placing Tone Marks in Pinyin

If there are two vowels in a syllable, as in the Chinese word hǎo (好), the ranking preference of where to place the tone mark is: a, e, o. If i and u appear together as the only two vowels in a syllable, you place the tone mark on whichever vowel comes last, as seen in the word jiǔ (九), or the word duì (对).

Tone Variations

Chapter 1 shows how the word 不 changes from a fourth tone pronunciation (bù) to a second tone pronunciation (bú) when it comes before another fourth tone syllable, such as in 不是 (bú shì). There are a few other syllables that also shift depending on the tone of the following syllable. For example, the character 一 (yī) is pronounced yì when followed by a first, second, or third tone syllable, as seen in 一天 (yì tiān), and is pronounced yí when followed by a fourth tone syllable, such as 一定 (yídìng).

Another rule is that you cannot say two third tone syllables in a row. So for words like 你好 (nǐ hǎo), the first third tone syllable is instead pronounced as a second tone (i.e., ní hǎo), even though the pinyin is still written with the two third tone marks.

Vocabulary Index (Chinese – English)

The Chinese–English Vocabulary Index is alphabetized according to pinyin. Words containing the same first Chinese character are grouped together. Words with the same pinyin spelling are organized according to their tone (that is, first tones first, second tones second, third tones third, fourth tones fourth, and neutral tones last).

Chinese	Pinyin	English	Page
		A	
啊	a	(word added at the end of a sentence to add emphasis or excitement)	137
		B	
八	bā	eight	19
爸爸	bàba	father, dad	57
吧	ba	(word added at the end of a sentence to make a suggestion or to soften the tone)	137
白大明	Bái Dàmíng	Daming Bai (a person's name)	31
北京	Běijīng	Beijing	89
本	běn	(measure word for books)	186
比赛	bǐsài	game, match, competition	118
不	bù	no, not	21
不太	bú tài	not really, not very	62
		C	
菜	cài	a dish (of food); cuisine; vegetables	205
场	chǎng	outdoor court or field (for sports)	114
吃	chī	to eat	205
宠物	chǒngwù	pet (animal)	67
吹	chuī	to blow, to play	133

Chinese	Pinyin	English	Page
		D	
打	dǎ	to hit, to play (basketball, ping-pong)	109
打电话	dǎ diànhuà	to make a phone call	205
的	de	(a possessive word that shows that something belongs to somebody)	31
笛子	dízi	flute	133
弟弟	dìdi	younger brother	57
点	diǎn	to order (food)	205
店	diàn	store, shop	137
电视	diànshì	television	62
电影	diànyǐng	movie, motion picture	158
都	dōu	all, both	84
对	duì	right, correct	84
多	duō	many, much, lots	216
		E	
而且	érqiě	and also	186
二	èr	two	18
二胡	èrhú	erhu	133
二十一	èrshíyī	twenty-one	163
		F	
饭馆	fànguǎn	restaurant	212
份	fèn	(measure word for a portion/serving of something)	212

Chinese	Pinyin	English	Page
		G	
哥哥	gēge	older brother	57
个	gè	(measure word for people and many everyday objects)	57
给	gěi	to give; for, to	205
狗	gǒu	dog	67
古筝	gǔzhēng	guzheng	133
馆	guǎn	indoor court or field (for sports)	118
贵	guì	expensive	186
		H	
还是	háishi	or (in questions)	89
好	hǎo	fine, good, nice; OK, it's settled	21
好吃	hǎochī	tasy, delicious	205
好看	hǎokàn	good-looking, nice-looking (used for people and things)	191
号	hào	day of the month	163
和	hé	and	41
很	hěn	very, really	62
红烧	hóngshāo	to braise in soy sauce (to red-cook)	212
后天	hòutiān	the day after tomorrow	158
会	huì	can, know how to	109
		J	
吉他	jítā	guitar	133
几	jǐ	how many	57

Chinese	Pinyin	English	Page
家	jiā	home	94
加油	jiā yóu	Do your best! Go! (shouted to cheer players on, literally means "add fuel")	118
简单	jiǎndān	simple	186
见	jiàn	to meet with, to see	182
件	jiàn	(measure word for clothing)	191
教	jiāo	to teach	141
饺子	jiǎozi	dumplings (with vegetable and/or meat filling)	212
叫	jiào	to be called	31
姐姐	jiějie	older sister	57
今天	jīntiān	today	158
经常	jīngcháng	frequently, often	118
九	jiǔ	nine	19
觉得	juéde	to feel, to think	114
		K	
看	kàn	to look at, to watch, to read, to see	62
可是	kěshì	but	62
可以	kěyǐ	can, could, may	141
快乐	kuàilè	happy	216
		L	
拉	lā	to pull, to play	133
篮球	lánqiú	basketball (the game and the object)	109
老师	lǎoshī	teacher	21
了	le	(a word that indicates an action is complete)	212

Chinese	Pinyin	English	Page
李	Lǐ	Li (surname, sometimes spelled Lee)	141
礼物	lǐwù	gift	168
两	liǎng	two (used when counting things)	59
林春月	Lín Chūnyuè	Isabella Lopez (a person's name)	37
林马丁	Lín Mǎdīng	Martin Lopez (a person's name)	37
六	liù	six	19
六月	liùyuè	June	163
		M	
妈妈	māma	mother, mom	57
吗	ma	(question word)	21
买	mǎi	to buy	137
卖	mài	to sell	137
猫	māo	cat	67
没有	méiyǒu	to not have	37
美国	Měiguó	United States of America	84
妹妹	mèimei	younger sister	57
面条	miàntiáo	noodles	212
明天	míngtiān	tomorrow	158
名字	míngzi	name	31
		N	
哪儿	nǎr	where	94
那	nà	that	89
那	nà	in that case, then, so	168

Chinese	Pinyin	English	Page
那儿	nàr	there, over there	114
难	nán	difficult	186
呢	ne	(word added at the end of a sentence to ask a follow-up question or to ask a question back to someone)	137
你	nǐ	you	21
你好	nǐ hǎo	hello	21
你们	nǐmen	you (plural)	41
		P	
朋友	péngyou	friend	41
便宜	piányi	cheap, inexpensive	186
乒乓球	pīngpāngqiú	ping-pong, table tennis; ping-pong ball	109
		Q	
七	qī	seven	19
去	qù	to go	114
		R	
人	rén	person, people	84
肉	ròu	meat (frequently pork)	212
		S	
三	sān	three	18
上午	shàngwǔ	morning (before noon)	182
谁	shéi	who	37
什么	shénme	what	31
生日	shēngrì	birthday	163

Chinese	Pinyin	English	Page
十	shí	ten	19
是	shì	to be	21
事	shì	thing, matter, something to do	182
书	shū	book	62
四	sì	four	18
送	sòng	to give (a gift)	191
所以	suǒyǐ	so, therefore	216
		T	
他	tā	he, him	37
她	tā	she, her	37
它	tā	it (used for animals and things)	67
他们	tāmen	they, them (if anyone in the group is male)	41
她们	tāmen	they, them (if everyone in the group is female)	41
弹	tán	to strum, to pluck, to play	133
踢	tī	to kick, to play (soccer)	109
听	tīng	to listen to, to hear	141
同学	tóngxué	classmate	37
同意	tóngyì	to agree	191
		W	
晚上	wǎnshàng	night, evening	182
网球	wǎngqiú	tennis; tennis ball	109
喂	wéi	hello (over the phone)	182
为什么	wèishénme	why	216

Chinese	Pinyin	English	Page
问	wèn	to ask (a question)	168
我	wǒ	I, me	21
我们	wǒmen	we, us	41
五	wǔ	five	19
		X	
喜欢	xǐhuan	to like	62
下个	xià ge	next	163
下午	xiàwǔ	afternoon	182
现在	xiànzài	now, at this time	94
想	xiǎng	to want (to do something)	114
小明	Xiǎomíng	(a name)	67
小区	xiǎoqū	neighborhood, apartment complex	94
谢谢	xièxie	thank you, thanks	141
星期	xīngqī	week	94
星期五	xīngqīwǔ	Friday	158
学	xué	to learn, to study	84
学生	xuéshēng	student	21
学校	xuéxiào	school	94
		Y	
颜色	yánsè	color	191
要	yào	to be going to (do something), to want (something; to do something)	182
也	yě	also, too, as well as	41
一	yī	one	18

Chinese	Pinyin	English	Page
一定	yídìng	certainly, definitely	168
衣服	yīfu	clothing	191
因为	yīnwèi	because	216
音乐	yīnyuè	music	141
英文	Yīngwén	English (language)	31
有	yǒu	to have	37
有	yǒu	there is, there are	114
有空	yǒu kòng	to have free time, to be free	158
有意思	yǒuyìsi	interesting, fun	114
月	yuè	month, moon	163
乐器	yuèqì	musical instrument	133
运动	yùndòng	sports, exercise	118
		Z	
在	zài	to be at, to be in (a place)	94
在	zài	at, in	118
再见	zàijiàn	goodbye, see you again	21
早上	zǎoshàng	early morning (until about 9:00 a.m.)	182
这	zhè	this	89
这儿	zhèr	here, over here	114
只	zhī	(measure word for some animals)	67
知道	zhīdào	to know	89
中国	Zhōngguó	China	84
中文	Zhōngwén	Chinese (language)	31

Chinese	Pinyin	English	Page
中午	zhōngwǔ	noon	182
种	zhǒng	(measure word for kinds, sorts, types)	205
周末	zhōumò	weekend	163
主意	zhǔyi	idea	168
祝	zhù	to wish (well)	216
昨天	zuótiān	yesterday	212
做	zuò	to do, to make	118
做菜	zuòcài	to make a dish (of food)	205
足球	zúqiú	soccer; soccer ball	109

Vocabulary Index (English – Chinese)

The English – Chinese Vocabulary Index is organized based on the alphabetical order of the English definitions.

English	Chinese	Pinyin	Page
A			
afternoon	下午	xiàwǔ	182
to agree	同意	tóngyì	191
all, both	都	dōu	84
also, too, as well as	也	yě	41
and	和	hé	41
and also	而且	érqiě	186
to ask (a question)	问	wèn	168
at, in	在	zài	118
B			
basketball (the game and the object)	篮球	lánqiú	109
to be	是	shì	21
to be at, to be in (a place)	在	zài	94
to be called	叫	jiào	31
to be going to (do something), to want (something; to do something)	要	yào	182
because	因为	yīnwèi	216
Beijing	北京	Běijīng	89
birthday	生日	shēngrì	163
to blow, to play	吹	chuī	133

English	Chinese	Pinyin	Page
book	书	shū	62
to braise in soy sauce (to red-cook)	红烧	hóngshāo	212
but	可是	kěshì	62
to buy	买	mǎi	137
C			
can, could, may	可以	kěyǐ	141
can, know how to	会	huì	109
cat	猫	māo	67
certainly, definitely	一定	yídìng	168
cheap, inexpensive	便宜	piányi	186
China	中国	Zhōngguó	84
Chinese (language)	中文	Zhōngwén	31
classmate	同学	tóngxué	37
clothing	衣服	yīfu	191
color	颜色	yánsè	191
D			
Daming Bai (a person's name)	白大明	Bái Dàmíng	31
day of the month	号	hào	163
difficult	难	nán	186
a dish (of food); cuisine; vegetables	菜	cài	205
to do, to make	做	zuò	118
Do your best! Go! (shouted to cheer players on, literally means "add fuel")	加油	jiā yóu	118
dog	狗	gǒu	67
dumplings (with vegetable and/or meat filling)	饺子	jiǎozi	212

English	Chinese	Pinyin	Page
E			
early morning (until about 9:00 a.m.)	早上	zǎoshàng	182
to eat	吃	chī	205
eight	八	bā	19
English (language)	英文	Yīngwén	31
erhu	二胡	èrhú	133
expensive	贵	guì	186
F			
father, dad	爸爸	bàba	57
to feel, to think	觉得	juéde	114
fine, good, nice; OK, it's settled	好	hǎo	21
five	五	wǔ	19
flute	笛子	dízi	133
four	四	sì	18
frequently, often	经常	jīngcháng	118
Friday	星期五	xīngqīwǔ	158
friend	朋友	péngyou	41
G			
game, match, competition	比赛	bǐsài	118
gift	礼物	lǐwù	168
to give (a gift)	送	sòng	191
to give; for, to	给	gěi	205
to go	去	qù	114

English	Chinese	Pinyin	Page
good-looking, nice-looking (used for people and things)	好看	hǎokàn	191
goodbye, see you again	再见	zàijiàn	21
guitar	吉他	jítā	133
guzheng	古筝	gǔzhēng	133
H			
happy	快乐	kuàilè	216
to have	有	yǒu	37
to have free time, to be free	有空	yǒu kòng	158
he, him	他	tā	37
hello	你好	nǐ hǎo	21
hello (over the phone)	喂	wéi	182
here, over here	这儿	zhèr	114
to hit, to play (basketball, ping-pong)	打	dǎ	109
home	家	jiā	94
how many	几	jǐ	57
I			
I, me	我	wǒ	21
idea	主意	zhǔyi	168
in that case, then, so	那	nà	168
indoor court or field (for playing sports)	馆	guǎn	118
interesting, fun	有意思	yǒuyìsi	114
Isabella Lopez (a person's name)	林春月	Lín Chūnyuè	37
it (used for animals and things)	它	tā	67

English	Chinese	Pinyin	Page
J			
June	六月	liùyuè	163
K			
to kick, to play (soccer)	踢	tī	109
to know	知道	zhīdào	89
L			
to learn, to study	学	xué	84
Li (surname, sometimes spelled Lee)	李	Lǐ	141
to like	喜欢	xǐhuan	62
to listen to, to hear	听	tīng	141
to look at, to watch, to read, to see	看	kàn	62
M			
to make a dish (of food)	做菜	zuòcài	205
to make a phone call	打电话	dǎ diànhuà	205
many, much, lots	多	duō	216
Martin Lopez (a person's name)	林马丁	Lín Mǎdīng	37
(measure word for books)	本	běn	186
(measure word for clothing)	件	jiàn	191
(measure word for kinds, sorts, types)	种	zhǒng	205
(measure word for people and many everyday objects)	个	gè	57
(measure word for a portion/serving of something)	份	fèn	212
(measure word for some animals)	只	zhī	67
meat (frequently pork)	肉	ròu	212

English	Chinese	Pinyin	Page
to meet with, to see	见	jiàn	182
month, moon	月	yuè	163
morning (before noon)	上午	shàngwǔ	182
mother, mom	妈妈	māma	57
movie, motion picture	电影	diànyǐng	158
music	音乐	yīnyuè	141
musical instrument	乐器	yuèqì	133
N			
name	名字	míngzi	31
(a name)	小明	Xiǎomíng	67
neighborhood, apartment complex	小区	xiǎoqū	94
next	下个	xià ge	163
night, evening	晚上	wǎnshàng	182
nine	九	jiǔ	19
no, not	不	bù	21
noodles	面条	miàntiáo	212
noon	中午	zhōngwǔ	182
to not have	没有	méiyǒu	37
not really, not very	不太	bú tài	62
now, at this time	现在	xiànzài	94
O			
older brother	哥哥	gēge	57
older sister	姐姐	jiějie	57

English	Chinese	Pinyin	Page
one	一	yī	18
or (in questions)	还是	háishi	89
to order (food)	点	diǎn	205
outdoor court or field (for sports)	场	chǎng	114
P			
person, people	人	rén	84
pet (animal)	宠物	chǒngwù	67
ping-pong, table tennis; ping-pong ball	乒乓球	pīngpāngqiú	109
(a possessive word that shows that something belongs to somebody)	的	de	31
to pull, to play	拉	lā	133
Q			
(question word)	吗	ma	21
R			
restaurant	饭馆	fànguǎn	212
right, correct	对	duì	84
S			
school	学校	xuéxiào	94
to sell	卖	mài	137
seven	七	qī	19
she, her	她	tā	37
simple	简单	jiǎndān	186
six	六	liù	19
so, therefore	所以	suǒyǐ	216

English	Chinese	Pinyin	Page
soccer; soccer ball	足球	zúqiú	109
sports, exercise	运动	yùndòng	118
store, shop	店	diàn	137
to strum, to pluck, to play	弹	tán	133
student	学生	xuéshēng	21
T			
tasy, delicious	好吃	hǎochī	205
to teach	教	jiāo	141
teacher	老师	lǎoshī	21
television	电视	diànshì	62
ten	十	shí	19
tennis; tennis ball	网球	wǎngqiú	109
thank you, thanks	谢谢	xièxie	141
that	那	nà	89
the day after tomorrow	后天	hòutiān	158
there is, there are	有	yǒu	114
there, over there	那儿	nàr	114
they, them (if anyone in the group is male)	他们	tāmen	41
they, them (if everyone in the group is female)	她们	tāmen	41
thing, matter, something to do	事	shì	182
this	这	zhè	89
three	三	sān	18
today	今天	jīntiān	158

English	Chinese	Pinyin	Page
tomorrow	明天	míngtiān	158
twenty-one	二十一	èrshíyī	163
two	二	èr	18
two (used when counting things)	两	liǎng	59
U			
United States of America	美国	Měiguó	84
V			
very, really	很	hěn	62
W			
to want (to do something)	想	xiǎng	114
we, us	我们	wǒmen	41
week	星期	xīngqī	94
weekend	周末	zhōumò	163
what	什么	shénme	31
where	哪儿	nǎr	94
who	谁	shéi	37
why	为什么	wèishénme	216
to wish (well)	祝	zhù	216
(word added at the end of a sentence to add emphasis or excitement)	啊	a	137
(word added at the end of a sentence to ask a follow-up question or to ask a question back to someone)	呢	ne	137
(word added at the end of a sentence to make a suggestion or to soften the tone)	吧	ba	137
(a word that indicates an action is complete)	了	le	212

English	Chinese	Pinyin	Page
	Y		
yesterday	昨天	zuótiān	212
you	你	nǐ	21
you (plural)	你们	nǐmen	41
younger brother	弟弟	dìdi	57
younger sister	妹妹	mèimei	57